## PURPLE ZONE

| | |
|---|---|
| A | VISITOR CENTRE |
| H | CAR PARK |
| 101 | 1940 DUNKIRK VETERANS' ASSOCIATION |
| 102 | SOLDIERS, SAILORS, AIRMEN AND FAMILIES ASSOCIATION |
| 103 | TWIN TOWERS MEMORIAL |
| 104 | WOMEN'S SECTION, ROYAL BRITISH LEGION |
| 105 | THE BRITISH BERLIN AIRLIFT MONUMENT |
| 106 | CADET FORCES GARDEN |
| 107 | AMBULANCE SERVICES |
| 107a | NORWEGIAN NAVY FLAGPOLES |
| 107b | DAVID CHILDS' TREES |
| 108 | THE QUEEN ALEXANDRA'S ROYAL ARMY NURSING CORPS |

## ORANGE ZONE

| | |
|---|---|
| B | THE CLOISTERS |
| C | THE MILLENNIUM CHAPEL OF PEACE AND FORGIVENESS |
| 201 | THE WAR WIDOWS' ROSE GARDEN |
| 202 | THE ST DUNSTAN'S PATHWAY |
| D | ST DUNSTAN'S MARKET SQUARE |
| 203 | GARDEN OF THE INNOCENTS |
| 204 | INTERNATIONAL MILITARY MUSIC SOCIETY |
| 205 | THE ARMY BENEVOLENT FUND – THE SOLDIERS' CHARITY |
| 206 | CHURCH LADS' & CHURCH GIRLS' BRIGADE |
| 206a | THE BOYS' BRIGADE |
| 207 | THE EX-NATIONAL SERVICEMEN'S MEMORIAL |
| 208 | AUXILIARY TERRITORIAL SERVICE STATUE |
| 209 | LICHFIELD & DISTRICT GARDEN |
| 210 | THE LEONARD CHESHIRE AMPHITHEATRE |
| 211 | THE BEVIN BOYS MEMORIAL |
| 212 | THE 'Y' GROUP MEMORIAL |
| 212a | OPERATION MARKET GARDEN/ MARKET GARDEN VETERANS' ASSOCIATION |
| 212b | 1ST AIRBORNE RECONN-AISSANCE SQUADRON |

## C

| | |
|---|---|
| 213 | |
| 214 | MEMORIAL |
| 215 | ROYAL AIR FORCE HALTON APPRENTICES MEMORIAL GARDEN |
| 216 | THE TREFOIL GUILD WILLOW SCULPTURES |
| 217 | BRITISH LIMBLESS EX-SERVICE MEN'S ASSOCIATION |
| 218 | THE ROYAL ARTILLERY GARDEN |
| 219 | THE INNER WHEEL GROVE |
| 220 | AUXILIARY TERRITORIAL SERVICE / ACK ACK |
| 221 | STILLBIRTH AND NEONATAL DEATH CHARITY MEMORIAL |
| 222 | ROYAL AIR FORCE REGIMENT |
| 223 | FIRE AND RESCUE SERVICES |
| 224 | WOMEN'S ROYAL ARMY CORPS |
| 225 | CIVIL DEFENCE |
| 226 | SUEZ VETERANS' ASSOCIATION |
| 227 | CHANGI LYCH GATE |
| G | THE FAR EAST PRISONERS OF WAR MEMORIAL BUILDING |
| 228 | THE SUMATRA RAILWAY |
| 229 | THE FAR EAST PRISONERS OF WAR GROVE |
| 230 | BURMA RAILWAY |
| 231 | THE CHINTHE WOMEN |
| 231a | ROYAL NORFOLK REGIMENT, SUFFOLK REGIMENT AND CAMBRIDGESHIRE REGIMENT MEMORIAL |
| 232 | BURMA STAR |
| 232a | THE CHINDIT MEMORIAL |
| 233 | THE IMPERIAL WAR MUSEUM PEACE GARDEN |
| 234 | THE ROTARY RIDGE |
| 235 | BRITISH KOREAN VETERANS |
| 236 | 17TH DOGRA REGIMENT |
| 237 | MALAYA & BORNEO VETERANS |
| 238 | ROYAL MALAYSIAN POLICE |
| 239 | MALAYAN VOLUNTEER FORCE |
| 240 | SULTAN OF OMAN'S ARMED FORCES |
| 241 | BALUCH REGIMENT |

## EEN ZONE

| | |
|---|---|
| | ARMED FORCES MEMORIAL |
| | NORMANDY VETERANS |
| | KING'S AFRICAN RIFLES |
| 303 | THE ROYAL ENGINEERS |
| 304 | THE FREEMASONS |
| 305 | THE BEAT (POLICE MEMORIAL AVENUE) |
| 306 | POLICE MEMORIAL GARDEN |
| 307 | THE POLAR BEAR MEMORIAL |
| 308 | BROTHERHOOD OF GREEK VETERANS CHAPEL |
| 309 | CAVALRY GROVE (CRESCENT) |
| 310 | THE PHANTOM MEMORIAL |
| 311 | THE ARMY PARADE |
| 311a | THE ROYAL GREEN JACKETS |
| 311b | 10TH ROYAL HUSSARS |
| 311c | 11TH HUSSARS (THE CHERRY PICKERS) |
| 312 | WAR WIDOWS' WOOD |
| 313 | MEDITERRANEAN CAMPAIGNS OF THE SECOND WORLD WAR |
| 313a | THE ARMY WOOD |
| 314 | ROYAL LOGISTIC CORPS |
| 315 | KENYA POLICE |
| 316 | ROYAL MILITARY POLICE ASSOCIATION |
| 317 | SOROPTIMIST INTERNATIONAL |
| 318 | BRITISH GERMAN FRIENDSHIP GARDEN |
| 319 | ANGLO-JAPANESE PEACE GROVE |
| 320 | CELEBRATION OF LIFE GROVE |
| 321 | IRAQ/AFGHANISTAN WILLOWS |
| 321a | BASRA MEMORIAL WALL |
| 322 | THE NAVY WOOD |
| 323 | THE BLUES AND ROYALS |
| 324 | ROYAL TANK REGIMENT |
| 325 | MERCIAN WOOD |
| 325a | ROYAL CORPS OF SIGNALS |
| 326 | IRISH INFANTRY GROVE |
| 327 | THE GOLDEN GROVE |
| 327a | POLISH FORCES WAR MEMORIAL |
| 328 | ROYAL ARMY MEDICAL CORPS |
| 329 | SHOT AT DAWN |
| 330 | LICHFIELD WOOD |
| 330a | THE SHOWMEN'S GUILD OF GREAT BRITAIN |
| 331 | KINGFISHER WOOD |

## GREEN ZONE CONTNUED

| | |
|---|---|
| 331a | ARMY APPRENTICE NATIONAL MEMORIAL |
| 332 | HOUSEHOLD DIVISION |
| 332a | ROYAL ELECTRICAL AND MECHANICAL ENGINEERS |
| 332b | LIGHT INFANTRY MEMORIAL |
| 333 | ROYAL AIR FORCE WOOD |
| 334 | ROYAL AIR FORCE CRANWELL APPRENTICES |
| 335 | ROYAL AIR FORCE BOY ENTRANTS |
| 336 | COASTAL COMMAND |
| 337 | ROYAL NATIONAL LIFEBOAT INSTITUTION |
| 337a | SHACKLETON ASSOCIATION MEMORIAL |
| 338 | THE 41 CLUB |
| 339 | ANCIENT BURIAL MOUND |
| 340 | THE ROYAL OBSERVER CORPS |
| 340a | ROYAL AIR FORCE ASSOCIATION REMEMBRANCE GARDEN |
| 341 | ROYAL & SUN ALLIANCE MEMORIALS |
| 341a | NO 30 SQUADRON ASSOCIATION |
| 342 | ROYAL AIR FORCE SERVICING COMMANDO AND TACTICAL SUPPLY WING ASSOCIATION |
| 343 | ROYAL AUXILIARY AIR FORCE |
| 343a | AIRCREW ASSOCIATION MEMORIAL |
| 344 | ROYAL AIR FORCE WING |
| 344a | THE ROYAL AIR FORCE POLICE |
| 345 | WOMEN'S AUXILIARY AIR FORCE |
| 346 | AIR FORMATION AND AIR SUPPORT SIGNALS |
| 346a | 90 SIGNALS UNIT |
| 347 | ROYAL AUSTRALIAN AIR FORCE |
| 348 | ADJUTANT GENERAL'S CORPS COMMEMORATIVE GARDEN |
| 349 | STAFFORDSHIRE REGIMENT |
| 350 | ASSOCIATION OF JEWISH EX-SERVICEMEN AND WOMEN |
| 350a | THE SHRIEVALTY AVENUE |
| 351 | GALLIPOLI |
| 352 | MERCIAN VOLUNTEERS |
| 353 | HOME SERVICE FORCE |
| 354 | TOC H |

## BLUE ZONE

| | |
|---|---|
| 401 | YEOMANRY AVENUE |
| 401a | BRITISH SOUTH AFRICA POLICE |
| 402 | ROYAL HONG KONG POLICE |
| 402a | NORTHERN RHODESIA POLICE MEMORIAL |
| 403 | BIDADARI CEMETERY |
| 403a | MEMORIAL FOR ST JOHN VOLUNTEERS |
| 404 | BLESMA EXTENSION |
| 405 | YANGTZE INCIDENT |
| 406 | ROYAL INDIAN NAVY AND INDIAN ARMY |
| 407 | FAR EAST AIR FORCE |
| 408 | DIAMOND GROVE |
| 409 | ROYAL NORWEGIAN NAVY |
| 409a | NATIONAL ASSOCIATION OF MEMORIAL MASONS |
| 410 | FLEET AIR ARM OFFICERS |
| 410a | ROYAL MARINES ASSOCIATION |
| 411 | BRITISH NUCLEAR TEST VETERANS |
| 411a | THE COMMANDOS |
| 411b | SHROPSHIRE YEOMANRY MEMORIAL PLINTH |
| 412 | THE ANTELOPE GARDEN |
| 413 | ROYAL NAVAL REVIEW |
| 413a | ROYAL NAVAL PATROL SERVICE |
| 414 | DEFENSIVELY EQUIPPED MERCHANT SHIPS |
| 415 | MASTER MARINERS SUNDIAL |
| 416 | THE MERCHANT NAVY CONVOY |
| 416a | ROYAL FLEET AUXILIARY SHIP 'SIR PERCIVALE' ANCHOR |
| 417 | WOMEN'S ROYAL NAVAL SERVICE |
| 417a | ARMY DOG UNIT (NORTHERN IRELAND) ASSOCIATION RED PAW |

## BLUE ZONE CONTINUED

| | |
|---|---|
| 417b | THE QUEEN ALEXANDRA'S ROYAL NAVAL NURSING SERVICE AND THE VOLUNTARY AID DETACHMENT (RN) |
| 418 | ULSTER SPECIAL CONSTABULARY |
| 418a | THE ROYAL BRITISH LEGION NATIONAL REMEMBRANCE GARDEN – 'MY REMEMBRANCE DAY' |
| 419 | ARMED SERVICES WOOD |
| 419a | DOUGLAS SKENE GROVE |
| 420 | THE ULSTER ASH GROVE |
| 420a | THE RUC GC WAY |
| 421 | THE HOME FRONT |
| 421a | THE NATIONAL EX-PRISONER OF WAR ASSOCIATION |
| 422 F | THE CHILDREN'S WOODLAND |
| 422a | THE EDWARDS TRUST GARDEN |
| 423 | FELLOWSHIP OF THE SERVICES |
| 424 | MILLENNIUM WOOD |
| 424a | WOMEN'S INSTITUTE |
| 425 | THE ROYAL BRITISH LEGION POPPY FIELD |
| 425a | THE SPIRITUALISTS NATIONAL UNION |
| 426 | RAC FUTURE FORESTS |
| 427 | THE ROADPEACE WOOD |
| 428 | ALLIED SPECIAL FORCES ASSOCIATION |
| 429 | WESTERN FRONT ASSOCIATION |
| 430 | UNITED NATIONS AVENUE |
| 431 | WATERSMEET |

Photo by Sue Elliott

# CONTENTS

The National Memorial Arboretum is the UK's year-round Centre of Remembrance; a spiritually uplifting place which honours the fallen, recognises service and sacrifice, and fosters pride in our country.

Our vision is to create a world-renowned Remembrance Centre worthy of those who give so much to our Country.

# ABOUT US

**The origins of the Arboretum can be traced back to a visit to Arlington Cemetery and the National Arboretum in Washington, DC, in 1988 by founder, David Childs. He had the idea that such concepts could be introduced to Great Britain to provide a meaningful memorial to those who have served since 1945. David Childs was greatly supported by Group Captain Leonard Cheshire VC CH DSO** DFC, who was concerned about future Remembrance and became influential in the concept of the Arboretum. The amphitheatre at the Arboretum is dedicated to his memory.**

The then Prime Minister John Major launched the appeal to create the Arboretum in November 1994. At this stage there was no land or money for the project but this quickly changed when Redland Aggregates (now Lafarge) generously gifted 82 acres of reclaimed gravel working alongside the banks of the River Tame. This generous gift has now been extended by a further 70 acres which includes the wildlife lake.

The Arboretum was officially opened by HRH The Duchess of Kent on 16 May 2001. The design was carefully conceived to provide both a space for peaceful contemplation and a living and growing environment for an assortment of trees and wildlife. Family members, friends and comrades can come and remember loved ones in a tranquil setting.

Located in the heart of the Nation, with 50,000 maturing trees and over 200 memorials, the National Memorial Arboretum is a beautiful and lasting tribute to those who serve their country or who have died in conflict.

# A RECLAIMED SITE

**265 million years ago central England was part of a vast, hot landscape of shallow lakes in red sandy desert. These conditions produced the red marl that forms the local 'bedrock' and gives the soil its distinctive red colour.**

Millions of years later, during the Ice Age, a drop in temperature led to the breaking up and grinding together of rocks by frost action, which is the repeated freezing and thawing of water in rock. During warmer periods meltwater rivers carried gravels from higher land to form the mineral deposits that are worked for aggregates today.

At the end of the ice age thin layers of finely grained sediment were deposited over the gravels to form the soils which enabled plants to grow and farming to take place.

The sand and gravel deposited in the Alrewas area thousands of years ago is quarried by Lafarge for use in construction throughout the region, including homes, schools, hospitals and roads. The land where the National Memorial Arboretum has been established was quarried in the late 1980s and early 1990s.

When the first phase of quarrying ceased, the land was restored using inert wastes such as soils and clays which cannot be recycled. The Arboretum's many groves have been established on this land.

Lafarge will continue to quarry at Alrewas until the work is finished, and will restore the land progressively. The company is proud to have played a part in the development of the Arboretum and surrounding countryside.

In October 2002, the skull of a 40,000 year old woolly rhino was found in Lafarge's Alrewas Quarry by digger driver Ray Davis. The woolly rhino lived during the middle part of the last major glaciation of the British region, about 30,000 to 60,000 years ago. Other finds at the quarry include remains of woolly mammoth, horse, bison and reindeer. Quarrying is important to archaeologists, who can quickly search for historical artefacts in large areas of land that are being quarried.

Photo by Lafarge Aggregates

# TREES

**Visitors to the National Memorial Arboretum can enjoy a wide variety of trees, many of which have a relevance to the memorials around them.**

Although still a 'young' Arboretum, there are already in excess of 50,000 trees in the grounds which are rapidly growing into a unique living tribute. The Beat is an avenue of London plane and some chestnuts which were funded by every Police Force in the UK. Chestnuts were chosen because the first truncheons were made from this extremely durable wood.

Visitors to the Chapel will be struck by the twelve pillars of Douglas fir. Construction of the Chapel began in 1999, the 200th anniversary of the birth of Scottish plant collector, David Douglas. Between 1825 and 1827 David Douglas travelled a staggering 10,000 miles in Western Canada and North West USA on foot and by canoe collecting and classifying plants. As a result of his efforts, 200 new plants were introduced to the UK, including the Douglas fir.

Six Dawn redwoods, Metasequoia glyptostrobides, can be found on the Ambulance Service plot. These magnificent trees, identified as a 'living fossil' in 1941, once blanketed the entire Northern Hemisphere and were thought to be extinct by Western botanists until their rediscovery in 1941 in the Szechuan Province of China.

At the end of The Beat can be found the Golden Grove which celebrates the lives of couples who married at the end of World War II and commemorated their 50th anniversary by dedicating trees. All the trees in the Grove have either golden leaves, fruits or stems such as the golden stemmed ash. At its centre is the magnificent Polish Armed Forces Memorial.

Passing through the Golden Grove you will come across a sinuous line of young redwoods planted by the International Tree Foundation. During the California Gold Rush in the 1850s, a prospector searching for gold stumbled into a grove of giant redwood trees – Sequoiadendron giganteum. These are the world's largest trees in terms of volume. The General Sherman Tree in Sequoia National Park, California, is nearly 84 metres high, with the first branch 40 metres above ground level, and weighs around 2,100 tonnes. One day, we hope, our trees will be this big!

Of the 33 truly native species found in the UK, such as black poplar and strawberry tree, 32 can be found at the Arboretum. The only one missing is Wych elm, which died as a result of Dutch elm disease.

## EXPLORE THE WORLD OF TREES

**A partnership has been created between the National Memorial Arboretum and Bedgebury Pinetum, Kent, which has the largest and most complete collection of temperate conifers in the world.**

Working with the Curator Chris Reynolds, and Propagator, Dan Luscombe, a simple system has been established where they can transfer to the Arboretum specimens of endangered trees such as the Chilean Plum Yew, Prumnopitys andina. It is important that we safeguard as many species of trees as possible as the loss of woodland cover worldwide is running at 200 square kilometres of forest a day, according to the Food and Agriculture Organisation of the United Nations.

In 2009 forest fires in Greece burned 21,000 hectares of pine forest in just four days. One of the species we have been given is Abies cephalonica, the Grecian fir, a species devastated by the fire. When our trees are big enough to produce cones we will be able to offer seed/seedlings for restocking areas of Greece where the species has been lost.

Another example, the Serbian spruce, is extremely rare in the wild and endemic to only one valley in western Serbia. Should this population be lost then arboreta like Bedgebury and the National Memorial Arboretum will be the only sites with specimens grown from wild-sourced seed whose own seed can be used to help prevent the species from becoming extinct. The trees we have planted will also have another role in that they will be used to educate people in the fields of arboriculture, conservation and environmental understanding.

## EXAMPLE OF A BOTANIC LABEL

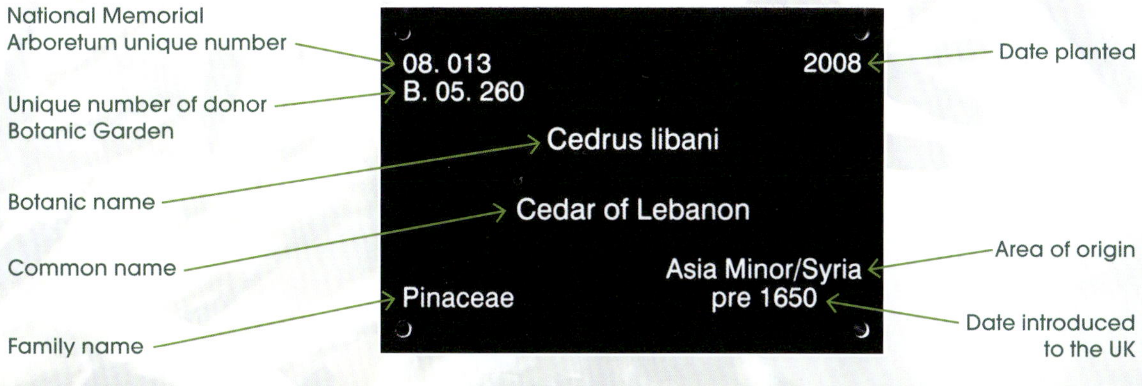

E Map reference

# ARMED FORCES MEMORIAL

## WHY THE MEMORIAL IS SO IMPORTANT

**The men and women of our Armed and Merchant Services who have lost their lives in conflict, as a result of terrorist action or on training exercises since the end of World War II are remembered here. Unlike the World War memorials in towns and villages across the Nation, there is nowhere else that records almost 16,000 names of those who have been killed on duty in recent times.**

Since 1945 the men and women of the Armed and Merchant Services have taken part in more than 50 operations and conflicts across the world, often as part of United Nations, NATO or other international coalitions. These actions have ranged from hot war to peacekeeping; from humanitarian assistance to fighting terrorism; from the jungles of Malaysia to the storms of the South Atlantic; from the seaport of Aden to the streets of Northern Ireland.

It is not just Service men and women who have made sacrifices. Behind every name on the Memorial there are the wives, husbands, partners, parents, children and colleagues who loved them and who live with the pain and consequences of their loss every day.

Photo by Nick Mott

Photo: copyright National Memorial Arboretum

## THE MEMORIAL

**The Armed Forces Memorial, dedicated in the presence of Her Majesty The Queen on 12 October 2007, is a nationally significant focus for Remembrance, providing recognition and thanks for those who have given their lives in the service of the country since the two World Wars.**

The Memorial is a stunning piece of architecture designed by Liam O'Connor which draws its inspiration from the ancient landscapes of prehistoric Britain and the classical forms of ancient Rome. It consists of a six metre high earth mound, 100 metres wide at the base reducing to just 50 metres wide at the top, which is based on early British barrows or tumuli. The spiral walkway up the grassy, tree-planted slopes provides accessibility to people of all ages and mobility. At the top of the mound stands a 43 metre diameter stone structure, comprising two curved walls and two straight walls which are constructed of 200,000 bricks faced with Portland stone panels.

The Memorial is particularly important for the many families and friends who have no grave to visit, or who remember those in graves in far-off places. The Memorial plays a valuable role in helping all who grieve for a Service person to come to terms with their loss, by providing a focus for their grief as they pass through different stages of their lives.

## THE SCULPTURES

**At the centrepiece of the Memorial are two evocative bronze sculptures, the embodiment of loss and sacrifice. Created by Ian Rank-Broadley, best known for his image of HM Queen Elizabeth II which has appeared on all UK and Commonwealth coinage since 1998, the sculptures bear silent witness to the cost of armed conflict. This significant new work is becoming an icon identifiable to all and especially to those who live with the consequences of the Nation's call to duty.**

## HOW THE NAMES ARE RECORDED

**The names of those who have died are recorded first of all by year, within each year by Service – Royal Navy, Army, Royal Air Force – and then in date order, so colleagues who died in the same incident are grouped together. Naming starts on the left circular wall as you enter the Memorial from the steps.**

To help you find a name quickly, you can look up the location of a relative or loved one by asking a member of our team at Reception. Every effort will be made to assist you with any queries.

**The theatres of conflict where the United Kingdom Armed Forces have served since World War II include:**

- Palestine 1945-1948
- Malaya 1948-1960
- Yangtze 1949
- Korea 1950-1953
- Canal Zone 1951-1954
- Kenya 1952-1956
- Cyprus 1955-1959
- Suez 1956
- Arabian Peninsula 1957-1960
- Congo 1960-1964
- Brunei 1962-1964
- Borneo 1962-1966
- Cyprus 1964 to present day
- Radfan 1964
- South Arabia 1964-1967
- Malay Peninsula 1964-1965
- Northern Ireland 1969-2007
- Dhofar 1969-1976
- Rhodesia 1979-1980
- South Atlantic 1982
- Lebanon 1983-1984
- Gulf of Suez 1984
- Gulf 1986-1989
- Peshawar 1989-1990
- Namibia 1989-1990
- Gulf 1990-1991
- Iraq/Kuwait 1991-2003
- Western Sahara 1991 to present day
- Northern Iraq/Southern Turkey 1991
- Iraq 1991-2003
- Cambodia 1991-1993
- Former Yugoslavia 1992-2002
- Sarajevo 1992-1996
- Georgia 1993 to present day
- Rwanda 1993-1996
- Angola 1997
- Croatia 1996-1998
- Kosovo 1998-2002
- Sierra Leone 1999-2002
- Congo 1999 to present day
- Kosovo 1999 to 2007
- East Timor 1999
- Ethiopia and Eritrea 2000 to present day
- Macedonia 2001-2002
- Afghanistan 2001 to present day
- Iraq 2003 to 2009
- Libya 2011

Map reference

# THE MILLENNIUM CHAPEL OF PEACE AND FORGIVENESS

**The Chapel welcomes all people from all faiths and walks of life. It is the spiritual hub of the Arboretum.**

The Chapel's wood construction is supported on twelve trunks of Douglas fir, each one representing one of the twelve apostles on whose witness the early church was built. Douglas fir was selected to pay tribute to David Douglas, the great plantsman, the 200th anniversary of whose birth coincided with the beginning of work on the Chapel. Each pillar has a carving by Jim Heath of one of the apostles.

The Chapel has no cornerstone reflecting the idea that "Christ is our cornerstone".

## THE MILLENNIUM PRAYER

**The desire to explore the true meaning of the Millennium that led to the building of the Chapel, led Lord Lloyd Webber to run a competition to create a Prayer for the Millennium. The winning prayer was written by 13 year-old Anna Crompton, from Ipswich. It is fitting that this prayer is now displayed on the front of the building to greet all our visitors. The carving was executed by Tom Staddon in cherry wood.**

## THE CANDLESTICKS

**The altar candlesticks were created by a local partnership between Arthur Price, the internationally reputed tableware Company, and Robert Carr, a Lichfield jeweller.**

The design links back to the altar being a table, most especially one connected with the Last Supper, at which the sacrament of communion was first celebrated. At that supper the one implement that every disciple would have had available was a knife. The pair of candlesticks thus represents the twelve knives of the apostles. They are bound by barbed wire as a reminder that people still starve as a result of war and imprisonment. The knife design is 'Silver Dawn' reflecting the spirit of hope at the start of the Millennium. The work was crafted by the silversmith Robert Pritcherd-Gordon.

## THE ALTAR CROSS

**The cross of oak and burr walnut was designed and created by Daniel Lacey of Buckinghamshire and donated by Barbara Roberts.**

## THE TOC H LAMP

**This 'Lamp of Maintenance', one of which is found in all Toc H houses, is a replica of the one on the Toc H plot on Millennium Avenue.**

## THE CRUCIFIXION

**The central cross is a copy of the Cross of Sacrifice which can be found in every Commonwealth War Graves Cemetery throughout the world. The text at the bottom of the cross can be found in the hymn "O God of Earth and Altar, Bow down and hear our cry" by G K Chesterton. The crosses of the thieves are made from elm from trees destroyed by Dutch Elm disease.**

## THE ALTAR

**In keeping with the spirit of the Chapel, the young offenders in Swinfen Hall Prison were invited to make the altar, lectern and pulpit. On the altar are carved two texts:**

"When I was in prison ye visited me" and

"Thy Father that seest in secret will reward thee openly"

(The carving is visible during the season of Lent when the altar cloth is removed)

## THE ALTAR CLOTH AND LECTERN AND PULPIT FRONTALS

**The altar cloth was commissioned by The Women's Section of The Royal British Legion with a design based on the theme taken from Revelations:**

"The leaves of the tree are for the healing of the nations"

This text appears also on the lectern frontal and its theme continues on the pulpit frontal which records the motto of the BBC:

"And nation shall speak peace unto nation"

## THE CAVENDISH CROSS

**The large lime wood cross mounted on the wall opposite the altar was carved by Ken Willoughby of the Essex Woodcarvers as a tribute to the life and work of Baroness (Sue) Ryder of Warsaw CMG and Group Captain Lord (Leonard) Cheshire VC OM DSO** DFC. It is based on a processional cross in St Mary's Church, Cavendish, Suffolk, Headquarters of the Sue Ryder Foundation.**

Baroness Ryder was a Trustee of the Arboretum until her death the day before the Chapel was dedicated.

## THE TWO MINUTE SILENCE

**From its first conception, it was felt that the Chapel should be the one place in the United Kingdom where the Two Minute Silence was observed every day of the year.**

To achieve this, an introduction to the Silence was recorded together with the Last Post and Reveille by the buglers of the Royal Marines.

At 11 o'clock every day a light shines onto the altar from the bearing and elevation of the sun at 11am on 11 November, Armistice Day. All those in the Chapel or amphitheatre at that time are invited to stop in silence and recall those who have lost their lives in conflict.

## DEDICATION

**The Chapel was dedicated by The Right Reverend Keith Sutton, the then Bishop of Lichfield, on 2 November 2000, All Souls Day.**

The congregation included many of those whose skills and vision had helped make the Chapel a tribute to 2,000 years of faith.

## THE STORYTELLER

**This wonderful wooden carving on the east side of the Chapel was carved by the Essex Woodcarvers.**

This work symbolises the link between the apostles represented on the pillars and the teachings of Christ today. The twelve young figures listening to the Storyteller have each of them the potential to become new apostles of the holy word. The children who modelled for the work are all friends of the carvers while the model for Christ himself was their local vicar.

# THE PURPLE ZONE

**Access:** The majority of these memorials are accessible from the car park and entrance area to the Visitor Centre of the National Memorial Arboretum.

**Terrain:** Mostly firm surface suitable for all abilities.

**Starting point:** Main entrance gate.

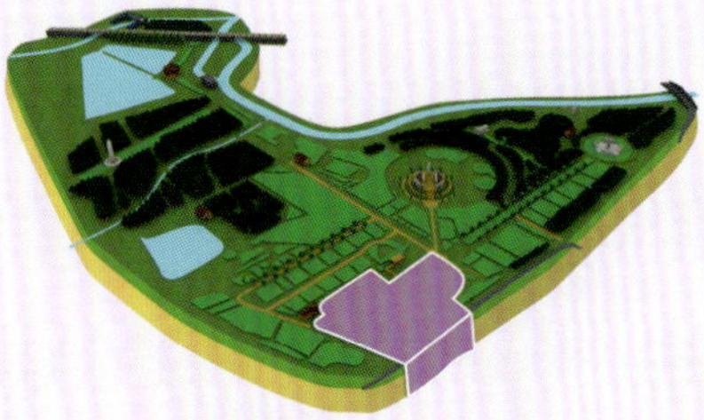

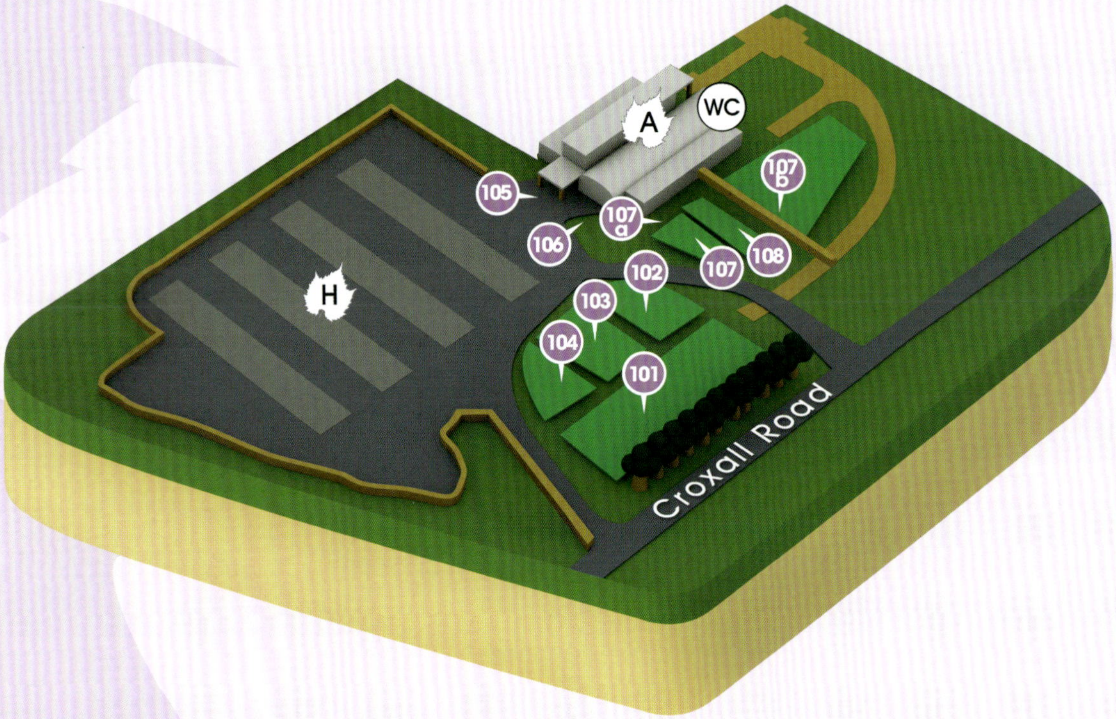

"THE SITE CAN LOOK FORWARD TO A VERY LONG, HEALTHY AND MUCH VISITED FUTURE. WE HOPE THAT YOU ENJOY YOUR VISIT AND TAKE MANY THOUGHTS AWAY WITH YOU."

David Childs, founder of the National Memorial Arboretum.

# 1940 DUNKIRK VETERANS' ASSOCIATION

**The avenue of Poplar trees, the seats and Memorial Plinth surrounded by sand brought from the beaches of Dunkirk was dedicated on 26 September 1999. The custom of using a rifle, boots, helmet and bayonet to mark a grave was used extensively during the American Civil War. During World War II, this custom was continued to mark the graves of fallen soldiers so the bodies could be recovered later. The rifle topped with a helmet has become known as the Battlefield Cross or Fallen Soldier's Cross.**

The memorial is a living tribute to all who took part in the operation code-named 'Dynamo', the evacuation of the Allied Armies from Dunkirk and neighbouring beaches between 26 May and 4 June 1940. During the course of the operation some 338,000 troops reached safety in England after being evacuated from Dunkirk and from beaches stretching 10 miles eastwards from the entrance to Dunkirk harbour. This evacuation was carried out by Royal Navy and Merchant Navy ships, aided by Allied ships and a mixed fleet of 'little ships'.

102

# SOLDIERS, SAILORS, AIRMEN AND FAMILIES ASSOCIATION

**Soldiers, Sailors, Airmen and Families Association (SSAFA) Forces Help has been serving the British Armed Forces and their families for over 100 years. Continually evolving support services are driven by the current needs of the Service community. In today's high pressure military environment, contemporary veterans, serving personnel and reservists alike often experience different problems from the soldiers, sailors and airmen of earlier conflicts.**

In 2010 SSAFA Forces Help celebrated 125 years of service to our Armed Forces. The memorial shows the SSAFA logo on a raised plinth.

103

# TWIN TOWERS MEMORIAL

**This international planting is a memorial to those who lost their lives in the terrorist attacks on the twin towers of the World Trade Centre in New York in 2001. The plaque in the memorial plinth contains debris from 'Ground Zero' that has been entrusted to us by the British Fire and Rescue Services and was donated by their counterparts in the USA.**

The memorial was dedicated on the first anniversary of the attack. The tree planting comprises two Giant redwoods representing the twin towers together with an English oak, a Scots pine, a Welsh yew, an Irish strawberry tree and an American black oak.

104

# WOMEN'S SECTION, ROYAL BRITISH LEGION

**The stone plinth, surrounding garden and benches are dedicated to members and friends of the Royal British Legion Women's Section and the memorial was opened on the 6 June 2005 by their National President HRH The Princess Royal. The three trees in the garden are maple, mountain ash and a three stemmed silver birch.**

105

# THE BRITISH BERLIN AIRLIFT MONUMENT

**This memorial and grove are in tribute to those who took part in the Berlin Airlift, the operation to deliver food and supplies to a besieged Berlin, between June 1948 and May 1949.**

The memorial plinth, created by the sculptor Andy de Comyn, is curved and has three ribs as a symbol of the three air lanes into Berlin from the French, British and American sectors of West Berlin. Members of the Essex Woodcarvers carved the life sized Golden Eagle which is coming in to land on top. The wood used is Iroko. The avenue of 39 fruit trees behind the plinth is planted to commemorate the lives of the 39 personnel lost during the airlift.

The feasibility of supplying two million Berliners by air alone was first proposed by RAF Air Commodore Rex Waite. As a result 2.326m tons of supplies were airlifted into Berlin. 31% was flown in on British aircraft in 175,000 flights involving over 30 million miles of flying.

106

# CADET FORCES GARDEN

**The circular seat with surrounding planting was sponsored by various Army Cadet Forces around the country through the initiative of the Staffordshire and West Midlands (North Section) Army Cadet Force. The planting is designed to take into account future global warming and has used species that grow in drier conditions such as senecios, phormiums and euphorbias. This is a particularly sunny area for visitors to sit and rest.**

In 2010, the Cadet Force's 150th anniversary year, a rededication service was held and a plaque placed in the paving was unveiled, honouring all those who have served.

107

# AMBULANCE SERVICES

**This garden was dedicated on 16 September 2004 and designed in the shape of an A – not only the initial letter of the service, but also to stand for 'Asclepius' the Greek God of healing and medicine.**

There are six prehistoric Dawn redwood trees to the right of the garden, and three rowan trees to the left. The significance of the rowan is that it was used to make the handles of stretchers in World War I . Other shrubs you will see around the garden are Skimmia japonica, Berberis darwinnii and dogwood, all used historically for healing.

The memorial garden has been created as a lasting tribute to all Ambulance personnel who have died but especially to those who have been killed on duty 'in service' to others.

## 107a

# NORWEGIAN NAVY FLAGPOLES

**Standing on the slope at the back of the Ambulance garden are three flagpoles which were donated by the Norwegian Navy.**

They also have a line of trees near to the Memorial Masons Grove.

## 107b

# DAVID CHILDS' TREES

**Two trees were planted to thank the founder of the Arboretum; one plaque reads The Founder's Tree. "To be remembered is o'er paid".**

Photo by OceanBarefoot

108

# THE QUEEN ALEXANDRA'S ROYAL ARMY NURSING CORPS

**Queen Alexandra's Imperial Military Nursing Service was founded in 1902, becoming Queen Alexandra's Royal Army Nursing Corps (QARANC) in 1949.**

The memorial sculpture and stone was designed by Ian H. Stewart and was a gift of the Corps to the future. The memorial was dedicated on 11 June 2002.

The short red capes that the Sisters wear are called 'tippets'. Queen Alexandra, the wife of King Edward VII chose the badge and insignia including the white cross from the flag of her native country, Denmark.

The QAs most notable veteran, for her service both during and after World War II, was Brigadier Dame Margot Turner DBE RRC. Surviving a direct hit on the SS Kuala and having been ordered to leave Singapore in February 1942 with other civilian and service women, she survived the shelling of two ships before being captured. She then spent three and a half years as a prisoner of war of the Japanese. She continued her career in the QAs after the War and was promoted to Matron-in-Chief and Director Army Nursing Services in 1964.

# THE ORANGE ZONE

**Access:** From the Long Gallery in the Visitor Centre.

**Terrain:** Mostly firm surface suitable for all abilities.

**Starting point:** Cloister Walkway.

"SEEING WHAT HAS HAPPENED TO THESE MEN AND WOMEN WE MUST NEVER FORGET THE SACRIFICES THEY HAVE MADE. A FITTING TRIBUTE TO THOSE WHO SUFFERED – MAY WE NEVER FORGET THEM ALL."

Taken from visitor comments book, FEPOW memorial building.

fter working on the Thai-Burma railway, artist Ronald Searle (right) spent more than a year in Changi before liberation. e described his drawings as 'the graffiti f a condemned man who found himself among the reprieved.'

*was always terrified that the Kempei-tai – the Japanese equivalent of the (German) Gestapo – vould stumble on my drawings. But they never did and my head stayed on my shoulders.*

Sapper Ronald Searle, Royal Engineers

# THE CLOISTERS

## THE ROSE GARDEN WALK

**The paviours set between the plain bricks in the walkway around the cloisters are laid down in celebration of an event or in memory of someone's life. The tributes are for individuals, clubs or associations, and friends, family or colleagues have sponsored them. The bricks and paviours are being laid all along the Rose Garden Walk and Chapel area. The path in front of the Garden of the Innocents is also part of the paved walk.**

## THE MEMORIAL PLAQUES ON THE CLOISTER WALLS

**The Insurance Company plaques are from Royal and Sun Alliance offices and commemorate personnel who lost their lives in the two World Wars. As offices were closed or relocated the plaques were gathered together into a memorial garden at the company head office and when this office was itself relocated Royal and Sun Alliance asked for them to be brought to the Arboretum. There are also two freestanding memorials just off Millennium Avenue. The company continues to cover all maintenance costs and insurance fees.**

The Shipping Line plaques are from P & O Shipping Line offices. As with the insurance company, P & O have relocated to new offices that do not provide suitable hanging space for the large plaques. P & O covered refurbishment and hanging costs in the Cloisters. The wooden plaque created by 'The Mouseman', Yorkshireman Robert Thompson, is an interesting and valuable one. Look for the woodcarver's well-known trademark mouse on the edge of the plaque.

There are also plaques remembering employees from the Vestey Group plc. The Vestey family, already importing foodstuffs from the United States of America, saw the need for chilled transport and created the Blue Star Line. This enabled them to import food, particularly beef, into the country from their own farms in South America and Australia. They expanded into the wholesale and retail business in the UK and are one of Britain's largest companies.

Other plaques include those from railway companies such as the London Midland & Scottish.

201

# THE WAR WIDOWS' ROSE GARDEN

**The Rose Garden has been planted as a tribute to the Nation's war widows who often endure great hardship, as well as emotional stress, through the loss of their husbands.**

The Rose Garden design has four sections and takes visitors along the terrible journey of bereavement through the colours of the roses. The emotional trip starts with the reds of anger, into the purples of despair, then passes through the gentler colours of quiet acceptance and finally into the yellows of happy memories. In the centre of the four sections is a water fountain, a symbol of life and hope.

Photo by OceanBarefoot

202

Photo: copyright National Memorial Arboretum

# THE ST DUNSTAN'S PATHWAY

**The St Dunstan's scented garden and pathway, lined with all-year-round fragrant shrubs, is designed to guide blind and visually impaired visitors across the cloister area to the Chapel. The pathway was sponsored by St Dunstan's, a charity providing lifelong care to blind ex-Service men and women.**

The herbs and plants have been chosen not only for their scent but also for their colour and, if our visitors without visual impairment look carefully, they will see eye shapes and colours lining the walkway. The central feature, inlaid in the walkway and surrounded by four stone benches, is a mosaic depicting the St Dunstan's crest. The mosaic, designed and created by the Craft Team at St Dunstan's Ovingdean Centre and a number of St Dunstaners, shows a beacon of light and shield, bringing to mind the hope and support offered by the organisation.

D Map reference

# ST DUNSTAN'S MARKET SQUARE

**Here visitors can find a very special gift of military memorabilia or fresh cut flowers and wreaths, or simply enjoy a coffee and a slice of cake overlooking the Arboretum landscape. A 'must visit' is Knick Knacks – our very own charity shop run by our volunteers.**

203

# GARDEN OF THE INNOCENTS

**The Garden of the Innocents, dedicated in 2004, is a memorial to all child victims of war and terrorism.**

The theme of the Garden is portrayed in green and white symbolising innocence, with raised beds in the shape of jigsaw pieces which do not fit together, symbolising the confusion and bewilderment children suffer through war and violence.

The central tree is an elder planted in memory of Anne Frank. The blossoms of the tree are cut each year on 12 June, the anniversary of Anne's birthday, so the tree never bears fruit, just as Anne herself was prevented from reaching maturity.

204

# INTERNATIONAL MILITARY MUSIC SOCIETY

**The International Military Music Society (IMMS) was formed in the United Kingdom in 1977 to promote interest in military music and now has branches worldwide.**

The memorial consists of block paving to the front of the Chapel overlooking the amphitheatre creating a stage for performances, and four plaques on the Chapel shutters, representing the Royal Marines Band Service, the Corps of Army Music, Royal Air Force Music Services and IMMS itself.

These plaques commemorate the incalculable number of bandsmen, drummers, pipers and buglers who lost their lives in the service of their country, and celebrate the courage and fortitude of those military musicians whose actions were recognised with awards for bravery.

## 205

# THE ARMY BENEVOLENT FUND – THE SOLDIERS' CHARITY

**The Army Benevolent Fund – The Soldiers' Charity (ABF) Memorial Rose Garden is the site of a number of tribute Rose Funds all of which represent loved ones who have served or who were part of the extended Army family. Some are young soldiers who were killed in peacetime activities or in action in Afghanistan and Iraq. The Rose Fund Tribute Book is held in the Millennium Chapel.**

In 2010 a new plinth was dedicated at the end of the rosebed.

## 206

# CHURCH LADS' & CHURCH GIRLS' BRIGADE

**The Church Lads' and Church Girls' Brigade sponsored the paved memorial garden beside the chapel which includes a plinth and benches and was dedicated on 22 June 2002. Members of the Brigade designed, built and planted it and continue to maintain it. The pathways between the planted areas form the shape of a Christian cross.**

22 Berberis shrubs represent the 22 members of the Brigade who have been awarded the Victoria Cross and the two rowan trees represent the Brigade's future because as they grow they will always be greater than the past.

## 206a

# THE BOYS' BRIGADE

**This garden, a grass rectangle with one corner curved, is bounded by a low hedge of field maple and box. At the entrance two pieces of 5,000 year old 'bog oak' donated by the Republic of Ireland and the Northern Ireland Districts depict the twin pillars of Religion and Discipline. A path winds down to a small patio area where visitors can sit on a bench, set on a bed of Portland stone.**

A large granite rock from Scotland, to which a real metal anchor is attached and inscribed with the chorus of The Boys' Brigade Hymn "Will your anchor hold?" occupies a prominent position as does a solid slate plinth from Wales in the centre of the patio.

In 2009 500 bulbs – 125 of each of standard daffodils, pheasant-eye narcissi, Tête-à-tête daffodils and blue grape hyacinths – were planted. The bulbs represent the 125 years of existence of The Boys' Brigade.

A time capsule, containing items from Boys' Brigade young people of 2009, has been buried in the garden.

## 207

# THE EX-NATIONAL SERVICEMEN'S MEMORIAL

**The memorial is dedicated to all who served their country as National Service men between 1939 and 1962. The memorial sculpture, made of green granite, was designed by Ian Stewart and represents the four cardinal points of the compass where National Service was performed. The memorial sculpture, garden and seating were dedicated on National Service Day, 29 June 2003. A commemorative Ex-National Servicemen's service and parade is held annually on the last Sunday in June.**

208

# AUXILIARY TERRITORIAL SERVICE STATUE

**The life-size statue of an Auxiliary Territorial Service (ATS) girl wearing basic khaki uniform was sponsored by the Auxiliary Territorial Service as a tribute to their members who played an important role in World War II from 1939 to 1945. Made up of volunteers who undertook six weeks of basic training, the ATS was formed in September 1938. By December 1939 there were 23,900 women aged between 19 – 23 years old in the service, peaking in 1943 at 212,500.**

The ATS was disbanded in 1949. During hostilities 335 members of the ATS were killed, 94 reported missing, 302 wounded and 20 became POWs. The statue is the work of Birmingham sculptor Andy Decomyn who used his wife Francesca as the model. It consists of a cementitous render over a reinforced concrete core. The appearance is similar to limestone and will withstand weathering and acid rain whilst also being vandal resistant.

## 209

# LICHFIELD & DISTRICT GARDEN

**The seat with a canopy in the centre of the plot represents the three spires of Lichfield Cathedral. Arranged around the seat is a planting of trees, one for each parish within the Lichfield District.**

The trees were sponsored by each parish and placed in the geographical position relative to Lichfield. Lichfield District Council sponsored the seating and garden.

## 210

# THE LEONARD CHESHIRE AMPHITHEATRE

**The amphitheatre located outside the Chapel is dedicated to the memory of Group Captain Leonard Cheshire VC CH DSO** DFC, the founder of the eponymous homes and services, whose concerns for future Remembrance influenced the concept of the National Memorial Arboretum. Chapel services are often relayed into the Amphitheatre, concerts are performed here and the 11am Act of Remembrance is broadcast into the Amphitheatre every day of the year. The copper beech trees planted at the far side were chosen because they were Lord Cheshire's favourite trees. HM The Queen and HRH Prince Philip planted the trees at each end of the Army Benevolent Fund rose bed outside the Chapel on 3 July 2002.**

### THE BELL

**Located on the raised bank of the Amphitheatre is a large brass bell donated by Les Wills, one of the Arboretum's volunteers, in memory of his wife Betty who served in the Women's Royal Naval Service (WRNS). The Bell started life on one of the Bedford Fire Appliances that were in use in the City of Birmingham during 1960/70 and was presented to Les Wills QFSM by the personnel at A1 Central, Birmingham, on his retirement from the West Midlands Fire Service in 1987 as Assistant Chief Fire Officer (Operations).**

The Bell now has a modern day purpose, similar to that of a 'curfew bell' in that it is rung daily shortly before the Arboretum's closing time.

211

# THE BEVIN BOYS MEMORIAL

**During World War II there was a shortage of skilled mine workers and between 1943 and 1948 nearly 48,000 young men known as the Bevin Boys, many of whom were conscripts, joined regular miners in their dirty, dangerous but essential work keeping the coal supplies flowing. If his National Registration number was drawn out, a conscript was sent down the mines. Life was hard and dangerous for these men and many lost their lives.**

Famous Bevin Boys have included Jimmy Saville, Eric Morecambe and Brian Rix, who left the RAF to join the Bevin Boys.

The Bevin Boys Association sponsored the bench and trees at the side of Millennium Avenue, and a tree planting ceremony to commemorate the 60th Anniversary of the Bevin Boys was held on 27 April 2003. The three planted trees represent the regions in which the Bevin Boys served: Narrow oak (England), Mountain ash (Wales) and Scots pine (Scotland).

212

# THE 'Y' GROUP MEMORIAL

**The paths in this plot are laid out to form the letter 'Y' with dedicated benches and memorials alongside. The inspiration for the memorial came from Joan Nicholls and a group of ATS ladies who served in the War Office 'Y' group at Beaumanor and other 'Y' stations from 1940 to 1945.**

The 'Y' Group, who were mainly women from the ATS, WRNS and WAAF, were given the title of Special Wireless Operators and the main 'Y' station was at Beaumanor Hall in Leicestershire. The job of these stations was to intercept the Enigma coded wireless transmissions which were passed on to the code breakers at Bletchley Park. The operators became very skilled at this task and were able to tell individual enemy operators from the way that they used their Morse keys, thus helping to track enemy unit movements across Europe. Historians have indicated that the work carried out by the wireless interceptors shortened the war by two years, although the work remained a secret until the 30 year condition of the Official Secrets Act was lifted in 1975. The memorial also pays tribute to other services engaged in wireless interception, and in the right hand corner of the garden is a bench dedicated to Colin Grazier, Tony Fasson and 16 year-old Tommy Brown. Grazier and Fasson won the George Cross and Brown, the George Medal, for their part in capturing the code books and documents.

212a

# OPERATION MARKET GARDEN/ MARKET GARDEN VETERANS' ASSOCIATION

**Operation Market Garden was the code name for an Allied operation which took place in September 1944 to secure a series of bridges over the major rivers of the German-occupied Netherlands. 'Market' was the code name of the airborne assault and 'Garden' the ground assault. A memorial plinth and plaque tell the story of the assault and the orange plaque alongside remembers the Dutch Underground and the assistance they gave the British and Allied troops during Market Garden.**

The Market Garden Veterans' Association was formed to recognise the contribution of ground troops who had fought their way from Normandy through France, Belgium and into Holland. There is also an Airborne Association. The Association celebrates Operation Market Garden every September in Holland.

212b

# 1ST AIRBORNE RECONNAISSANCE SQUADRON

**In 1941 The Army Council decided to set up the Reconnaissance Corps. By June 1942 every division of the British Army had its own reconnaissance regiment whose motto was "Only the enemy in front, every other beggar behind".**

The small black Scottish granite memorial is dedicated to the men of the 1st Airborne Reconnaissance Squadron known as the Freddie Gough Squadron.

# GENERAL POST OFFICE MEMORIAL GARDEN

**The recent renovation of this garden was carried out by volunteers from Royal Mail Group (RMG). The path is laid out to replicate the Royal Mail insignia in the shape of a cruciform.**

The EIIR boxes come from the years 1952-1991. The words 'Royal Mail' first appeared on a British pillar box in 1991, reflecting organisational changes in the business. All the boxes have the relevant sovereign crowns depicted. The Edward VII box is 1901-1910, just before World War I and the George VI box is from around 1940, during World War II.

The green Victorian wall box came into service between 1871 and 1901. The one on display was bomb damaged during the blitz when it was blown out of a wall in Deptford, East London. The local people then rebuilt a wall around the box to keep it in service.

This memorial is a tribute to the thousands of employees who died or were wounded, to families who suffered, and to all Post Office people who worked steadfastly to keep services going through the turmoil and tragedy of war. Messages in letters, telegrams and telephone calls became vital lifelines for anxious relatives and friends at home and a medium of support to those on the battlefields. Also remembered are those who are still serving in the Territorial Armies around the world today.

## THE POST OFFICE DURING WORLD WAR I

**The Post Office had its own regiment from 1868, but to accommodate the swell of recruits in World War I a second Post Office Rifles (PORs) Battalion was formed in September 1914. Post Office Riflemen fought at Ypres and at Passchendaele and were involved in some of the worst carnage of the war at the Battle of the Somme. For their part, the PORs entered the hostilities late in the day (October) but still sustained forty dead, 160 wounded and some 200 missing.**

The Divisional General, on parade after an attack said "I thought you were a lot of stamp lickers, but the way you fought… you went over like a lot of savages". The Post Office Rifles received 145 awards for gallantry including one Victoria Cross. During 1917 over 19,000 bags of mail per day were sent to the troops in France. In the ten day period before Christmas Day, half a million bags of mail were sent to France.

Photo by OceanBarefoot

## THE POST OFFICE DURING WORLD WAR II

**Bomb-damaged Post Offices were supplemented by 'tented' Post Offices. In one night in September 1940, 23 London Post Offices were bombed. Staff often worked on despite air raid warnings. Afterwards broken glass, water, sewage and electricity mains were major hazards as thousands of telephone cables had to be repaired or rerouted.**

In December 1940, the Central Telegraph Office was damaged by bombs. Replacement facilities were operating within 48 hours.

**Radio broadcast from the General Post Office**

" You may know a good deal about the difficulties of the black-out, but I wonder if you know quite as much about it as the postmen who are making sure that your mail gets through…but this can only be done if you will help us by posting early and by early I mean before you go to lunch at noon to 1 o'clock… and when you are in your shelters I hope you will remember that the letters you posted…are being handled by postal and railway workers who still carry on in spite of barrage, blitzkrieg and black-out…This war has changed a great many things and it doesn't seem too much to ask that you should change your postal habits. Remember, post your letters every day before you go to lunch."

## THE POST OFFICE'S ROLE IN D-DAY

**The D-Day invasion force relied on communication lines installed by GPO engineers. As Sir Thomas Gardiner, Director General of The Post Office writes: "The telegraph network …was three times as extensive as the whole pre-war civil telegraph network. Nearly 60,000 telephone circuits had been provided for the use of the Forces. The mileage of trunk telephone lines made available to them was greater than that of the whole trunk network available for public use at the outbreak of war."**

After D-Day in June 1944 General Eisenhower wrote to the Postmaster General: "The build up of the necessary forces for the current operations has involved the construction of a vast network of communications radiating from the key centres of vital importance in the United Kingdom. The greater part of this work has been undertaken by the Engineers and Staff of the General Post Office. It is my great pleasure, on behalf of the Allied Expeditionary Force, to ask you to pass on to them my sincere appreciation for their contribution and for the long hours they have worked and for the excellent cooperation they have given toward our success."

**Communication with Prisoners of War (POWs) and civilians in Japan and Japanese occupied territories**

"Under Japanese regulations communications are limited to 25 words and must be typewritten or written clearly in block lettering… Only relatives and close friends should write, and no one family should write more than once a fortnight to the same prisoner. These restrictions are in the interests of the prisoners: it is to be assumed that comparatively few English-reading censors are available to the Japanese authorities and the delay in censorship abroad is certain to be considerable if letters… are too numerous."

214

# THE FAULD EXPLOSION MEMORIAL

**In November 1944 an estimated 4,000 tons of bombs and ammunition, stored in a Gypsum mine were accidentally detonated, killing seventy people including army personnel, Italian Prisoners of War who were working in the ammunition factory, and local residents and workers.**

It is believed that this site remains the largest single explosion caused by conventional weapons in both war and peacetime.

The explosion crater is situated about half a mile to the east of The Cock Inn at Hanbury, Staffordshire about twelve miles from the Arboretum. In 1990 a granite memorial to those who lost their lives was erected near the crater, having been donated by an Italian firm. The crater is clearly visible to walkers and visitors to the area, but its true depth of over 100ft has gradually been decreased as trees and other vegetation have grown as the years have gone by.

215

# ROYAL AIR FORCE HALTON APPRENTICES MEMORIAL GARDEN

**The association between the Halton House estate in Buckinghamshire and the RAF began in autumn 1912, when forces from Aldershot needed somewhere to practise the defence of London using their three aircraft and an airship.**

Today RAF Halton is a major RAF training establishment. The centrepiece of the garden represents the RAF Apprentice wheel badge. The tree to the left of the stone is dedicated to Thomas Gray, posthumous winner of the Victoria Cross, awarded in 1915 for coolness and resource while navigating the leading aircraft under most difficult conditions on a mission to destroy a bridge that was allowing German forces to cross into Belgium.

216

# THE TREFOIL GUILD WILLOW SCULPTURES

**The Trefoil Guild, a corporate member of Girlguiding since 2007, was formed as far back as 1920 for ex-Guides who wished to continue supporting Guiding and meeting old friends.**

Presently there are over 1,100 Guilds in the UK with a membership of over 20,000. Guilds support Guiding with starter packs for new units and financial help for Girlguiding members working and travelling abroad. They enjoy social events of their own and give practical help to Guiding and Scouting and their own community.

The Royal Family has always been closely connected with Guiding. HM The Queen, now Girlguiding's Patron, and the late Princess Margaret, became members in childhood. The late Queen Mother was Trefoil Guild Patron from 1960 until her death.

The willows in the garden have been planted and woven into the shape of the three leaves and stalk of the Trefoil, the badge of the Trefoil Guild and of Girlguiding.

217

# BRITISH LIMBLESS EX-SERVICE MEN'S ASSOCIATION

**The British Limbless Ex-Service Men's Association (BLESMA) was formed by various groups of severely disabled amputees trying to adjust to life in the so called, "land fit for heroes" in the years just after the Great War.**

In 1932 they all came together and the Association was formed. The fellowship of shared experience and the desire to get things done and to get things changed has always driven the Association.

Today, BLESMA still supports many veterans who lost limbs in World War II and in conflicts thereafter, offering its special skills to a new generation of young men and women disabled in the service of our country. BLESMA's youngest member to date has been 19 years-old – its oldest 99 years-old.

The fruit trees are kept at a low height to allow fruit to be picked from wheelchairs.

# THE ROYAL ARTILLERY GARDEN

**The Royal Artillery (RA) dates back to the eighteenth century and by the end of World War II had become larger than the Royal Navy. The modern RA uses a variety of equipment designed to fulfil a wide range of roles.**

This pleasant garden with its waterfall, range of planting and seats in the form of old gun carriages, owes its design and creation to the energies of Ray Hutchins, a local artist and former member of the Royal Artillery, and was created and subsequently maintained by Association members themselves. The alder tree planted on the island in the centre of the water feature is doubly significant, as alder charcoal was once used in the production of gunpowder and the name Alrewas is derived from 'alder wash', the alders in the river/wash. Around the garden and on the banking are trees dedicated to the Royal Artillery.

A few famous names associated with the RA:

- Spike Milligan (comedian)
- Orde Wingate (inspirational leader)
- Anthony Quayle (actor)
- Edward Heath (Prime Minister)
- E H Shepard (illustrator)
- Frankie Howerd (comedian)
- Sir Denis Thatcher (husband of Prime Minister)

**W.O. I (Regimental Sergeant Major) George WEST 94 Field Regiment RA.**

"On 14 May, 1945, a road patrol of 94 Field Regiment Royal Artillery reported a large half-buried bomb by the side of the main road in Basra and Regimental Sergeant Major West was sent to investigate the report. He found the bomb to be a one thousand pound sea-mine with a six day clock firing device. He unscrewed this firing device and made the mine harmless. This Warrant Officer fully appreciated the importance of the Second Army Supply route and, without thought of his own safety, he showed devotion to duty of the highest order. His cold calculating courage, in risking his life on six successive occasions, is beyond praise. The award of the George Medal was published in London Gazette, 5 October 1945."

## 219

# THE INNER WHEEL GROVE

**Inner Wheel was founded in Manchester in 1924. Its members are the female spouses, partners and relatives of Rotary International members. As the movement spread, International Inner Wheel was formed in 1967. Its aims are to promote true friendship, encourage the ideals of personal service and foster international understanding.**

The design of the Grove is based on the Inner Wheel Badge and echoes the gold and blue cogwheels in the trees and shrubs. In autumn 2008, the entrance to the Grove was enhanced by the erection of wrought iron gates, which were dedicated in March 2009.

## 220

# AUXILIARY TERRITORIAL SERVICE / ACK ACK

**It is fitting that the ladies who manned the anti-aircraft guns in World War II, the Auxiliary Territorial Service / ACK ACK (ATS / ACK ACK), who were members of the Royal Artillery, should have their plot next to the RA. The driving force behind this plot was Mrs Vee Robinson who is a veteran of the organisation.**

She visited a quarry on several blasting days until she found the rock that is placed in the centre of the plot. The shape reminds us of the angle of the search lights and guns which the ATS / Ack Ack girls worked with, and there is a poem and dedication engraved on the back of the stone. The plot was dedicated on 28 July 2000 at a ceremony attended by Lady Soames, the daughter of Sir Winston Churchill. The garden includes red flowering Malus planted over blue shrubs, the colours of the RA, and the Leylandii 'Robinson's Gold' in one corner is a tribute to Vee Robinson.

221

# STILLBIRTH AND NEONATAL DEATH CHARITY MEMORIAL

**Stillbirth and Neonatal Death Charity Memorial (SANDS) was founded in 1978. It was set up by a small group of bereaved parents devastated by the death of their babies and by a complete lack of acknowledgement and understanding of the significance and impact of their loss.**

SANDS aims to support anyone affected by the death of a baby; to work with health professionals to improve the quality of care and services provided to bereaved parents and their families and to promote changes in antenatal practice and fund research that could help to reduce the loss of babies' lives.

The SANDS Garden was designed by Nicholas Newton to reflect the emotional journey that many parents face in trying to come to terms with their bereavement. At the heart of the garden is a sculpture of the SANDS tear drop insignia which was created by John Roberts and the Portland Sculpture Trust to encourage adults and children to sit and touch the central carved figure of the baby. Two benches individually carved by Nigel Ross from reclaimed elm have been placed nearby.

222

# ROYAL AIR FORCE REGIMENT

**The Royal Air Force (RAF) Regiment provides specialist Force Protection for military airbases worldwide, and is a unique Corps within the RAF. It has been on operations constantly since World War II. HM The Queen is Air Commodore in Chief of the RAF Regiment.**

The RAF Regiment was formed on the prompting of Sir Winston Churchill and by the Royal Warrant of His Majesty King George VI in 1942. However, its roots go back to the 1920s when the RAF Armoured Car Companies were formed to protect the RAF assets exercising Air Control in the Middle East. Since its inception, it has fought in every major conflict and operational theatre, gaining a world-renowned reputation for its professionalism and expertise.

The RAF Regiment's Memorial Garden was dedicated on 5 April 2001 and the stark but impressive black granite memorial stone commemorates the worldwide service and sacrifice of Corps members since 1942. The shape of the paved area represents a landing strip and the grouping of the four Prunus amanogawa in each corner represents the four corners of the world in which the Corps serves. The Corps motto is "Per Ardua"; translated it reads, "Through Adversity".

223

Photo by David Paul

# FIRE AND RESCUE SERVICES

**The monument, 'Fire-fighters Serving Humanity', is a six and half ton block of red granite, surmounted by a stainless steel and enamel badge and engraved on both sides. It recognises the qualities of operational fire and rescue service personnel, past, present and future, who serve all the communities of our Nation.**

The eight points or tenets of the star depicted on the Monument represent the qualities required of a fire-fighter:

TACT – GALLANTRY – DEXTERITY – OBSERVATION – PERSEVERANCE – LOYALTY – EXPLICITNESS – SYMPATHY

## 224

# WOMEN'S ROYAL ARMY CORPS

**The Women's Royal Army Corps (WRAC) and its predecessors the Women's Army Auxiliary Corps, Queen Mary's Army Auxiliary Corps and the Auxiliary Territorial Service are remembered here.**

The front of the grove is based on the letter 'W' for women and behind is a more open area for seating and contemplation. The trees and shrubs planted were specially selected for their grace and elegance and also with three themes in mind: the bottle green of the WRAC uniform, the Corps Air "The Nut Brown Maid" or the connection with women's names.

Between 1917 and 1992, nearly half a million women joined the corps serving in every continent in over 35 trades with more than 1,200 dying in service.

## 225

# CIVIL DEFENCE

**The large central memorial stone commemorates the 1,900,000 who served in the Civil Defence Services during World War II and the nearly 7,000 who were killed. Their names and details are recorded in the Book of Remembrance lodged in the Chapel.**

The smaller stone reminds us of the service given by animals, both those working and those simply helping to maintain the morale of their owners. The plot was dedicated in June 2001.

To the right of the path to the centre is a tree dedicated in 2007 to those who were awarded the George Cross for Civil Defence service.

At the far end is the memorial to the volunteer service given by the (350,000 at any one time) Civil Defence Corps and the Auxiliary Fire Service between 1949 and 1968 during the height of the cold war. It was unveiled in 2008 by HRH The Duke of Gloucester.

Photo by David Faul

226

# SUEZ VETERANS' ASSOCIATION

**The aims of the Association, formed in April 1997, are to 'Rekindle and promote a spirit of comradeship amongst those who served in the Canal Zone, to organise periodic visits to the Canal Zone, to organise periodic reunions in the UK and to keep members informed of activities by means of a quarterly Newsletter'.**

From 16 October 1951 to 19 October 1954 British presence in Suez was without a treaty which the Egyptians had abrogated. That period became known as the 'Emergency Period' when service personnel were deemed to be 'On Active Service'. This service was not recognised by the award of the General Service Medal until June 2003, some 50 years later, and after a vigorous campaign.

**Britain's Small Wars – Suez Canal Zone (1951-1954)**

The Suez crisis of 1956 is often viewed as a major focus of post-war political history. Less well-known, certainly among the wider British public, were the years of conflict that preceded it. It was from those earlier years that the roots of the 'Suez Crisis' were sown in the towns and villages of the Suez Canal Zone in what became known as the 'Egyptian Emergency' of 1951-54.

The Canal Zone was known as 'the worst posting in the world' and the British Armed Forces (about a third of whom were RAF personnel) stationed there were mainly conscripts of National Service. The hostile climate, primitive sanitation, diseases and poor food all combined to make life very unpleasant. As if this was not enough, Egyptian terrorists began murderous attacks upon servicemen and their families, army camps, airfields and installations, all of which necessitated round-the-clock guard and escort duties. Ambushes, stabbings, abductions and murder became part of the terrorists' modus operandi.

By the time the Anglo-Egyptian agreement ended the conflict in 1954, the number of post-war casualties accounted for some 1,400 lives. Successive British governments always played down this part of history, effectively stifling the claim of Canal Zone veterans for the award of a Campaign Medal to mark that operation. It took 50 years of campaigning before veterans finally received the Canal Zone Medal.

# CHANGI LYCH GATE

**This is the original Lych Gate from Changi Jail, Singapore, designed by Captain C.D. Pickersgill and built in 1942 by men from the 18th Division who were prisoners of war.**

The gate was first erected at the entrance to the camp cemetery to mark the graves of those who had died and to give their funerals some dignity. In 1952 the graves were moved to Kranji War Memorial Cemetery and the Lych Gate to the British Garrison Church in Singapore. When British troops withdrew completely from Singapore in 1971, the Lych Gate was dismantled and brought back to England where it was erected at the Queen's Division Depot, Bassingbourn Barracks in Royston, Hertfordshire. In 2003 the refurbished Lych Gate was reconstructed at the Arboretum by the 39th Engineering Regiment and the re-dedication took place on 8 February 2004.

# THE FAR EAST PRISONERS OF WAR MEMORIAL BUILDING

**On 16 December 1994 an article in a local newspaper made an incredible impact on one woman who read it, so much so that three years later it brought about the beginning of COFEPOW – The Children (& Families) of the Far East Prisoners of War.**

As Carol Cooper from Norfolk started to read the newspaper article she realised with a tremendous shock that the soldier concerned was her father, a father who was sent to war when she was two years old.

The members of COFEPOW are the children and families of many thousands of men who died on the Thai/Burma railway, the Sumatra railway, the Sandakan Death Marches, in copper mines in Formosa, steel factories in Japan, building roads in Burma and air strips on Ambon, Haruka, Java, Rabaul, New Guinea and the Solomons. Thousands died on the 'Hellships', battened down in holds of unmarked ships and torpedoed by Allied submarines. In addition, thousands were captured and died when Hong Kong fell to the Japanese in December 1941.

The incarceration was not restricted to service personnel – many of the Far East prisoners were civilian internees.

Thousands survived to return after the war and for them the suffering continued for years after. Many of the Association's members bear testament to their fathers' constant nightmares and recurring illnesses.

COFEPOW established the Far East Prisoners of War Memorial Building, not only to remember those who died, but also to encompass the whole story of events during this unprecedented chapter in British history. The memorial roll contains the name and rank of all British Servicemen taken prisoner during the South East Asia conflict and embraces the story of their treatment and the thousands who died as a result.

The Java Memorial is two specially commissioned painted windows, replicas of the two made by Lt Cdr Upton, RNVR, for the tiny St George's church, built by the Prisoners of War (POWs) at Tandjong Priok. The original windows were saved after the war and are now on permanent display at the Anglican Church of All Saints in Jakarta. The replicas form a memorial to not only all those held at Tandjong Priok but also all who were taken prisoner by the Japanese and held captive in Java.

The Far East Prisoners of War Memorial Building was officially opened on 15 August 2005, the 60th anniversary of the end of World War II in the Far East.

far east
prisoners
of war
1941–1945

228

# THE SUMATRA RAILWAY

**The Sumatra Railway was constructed in extreme conditions on and around the Equator by 5,000 Allied prisoners of war (POW) and 30,000 local people. The railway was finished on 15 August 1945 (now known as VJ Day), so it was never used except to transport the prisoners on their journey home, and within a very short time it had disappeared back into the bamboo. Jack Plant, a veteran who worked on the railway, was inspired to construct the memorial by a sketch drawn by fellow POW Owen Greenwood, showing a stretch of the Railway under construction. The memorial remembers those who died, and asks for peace and reconciliation.**

Through the co-operation and generosity of many specialised firms, the memorial itself is made from material sourced in the UK, including replicas of the telegraph wires that were placed along the railway and the correct type of (British) rail tracks. Along the track are tools used in the original construction. The wording and illustrations on the brick memorial plinth describe the conditions and dangers that were endured by the prisoners. On both sides of the railway European and Japanese maple, rowan and cherry trees have been planted.

## JOURNEY ABOARD A JAPANESE 'HELLSHIP' BY JACK PLANT EX RAF 1940-1946

**"Early in 1943, a party of British RAF and Dutch personnel were lined up in an open area of Jaamarkt for what was said to be a medical inspection to determine who was fit enough to be put on a draft overseas. The 'medical' was, to say the least, perfunctory.**

We were lined up Tenko fashion and instructed to drop our pants; in that most of us were wearing shorts this presented no problem. Then along came a Japanese doctor, he was at least wearing a stethoscope and a white coat!

The following day thousands were called out on parade and each handed a small bag holding about half a kilo of uncooked rice; cursory examination showed the contents to be very poor quality and full of weevils. We were then marched down to Tanjong Perak, the docks in Soerabaya. Two ships were tied up alongside, we could see their names beneath a rough covering of paint, the Amagi Maru and the Matsukawa Maru. Despite the awful brutality to get us aboard quickly we lay alongside the dock for two or three days. Conditions, because of the heat, meant that life was almost intolerable.

After suffering for almost two weeks and a thousand miles we arrived at the port of Ambon on the island of Ambonia. Those POWs who claimed they could swim were allowed on deck to transfer stores from the ship to the beach. After that, we set sail again to our destination the island of Harulu a beautiful coral spice island. It was raining when we went ashore and there were no shelters, so we lay in the open in the rain all night."

## JUDY – WHO WAS SHE?

**'Judy' was a pure bred English Pointer, a Royal Navy mascot who got herself marooned off Sumatra (Dutch East Indies) during 1942.**

A young Airman named Frank Williams took to her and she to him. He became a Japanese POW but she never left him and stayed with him the whole time. Frank used to feed her, giving up a portion of his small ration of rice. Occasionally she would slip out of camp and get hold of food for herself. It was on one such occasion that she got herself pregnant and duly produced the puppies. The Japanese Camp Commander had one for himself.

She survived gunshot rounds, alligator bites, attacks from wild dogs and from a tiger seeing her through to August 1945 when Frank was released.

On return to the UK she was awarded the Dogs VC for bravery (The Dickin Medal). The book about Judy, written by E Varley is called 'Judy VC'.

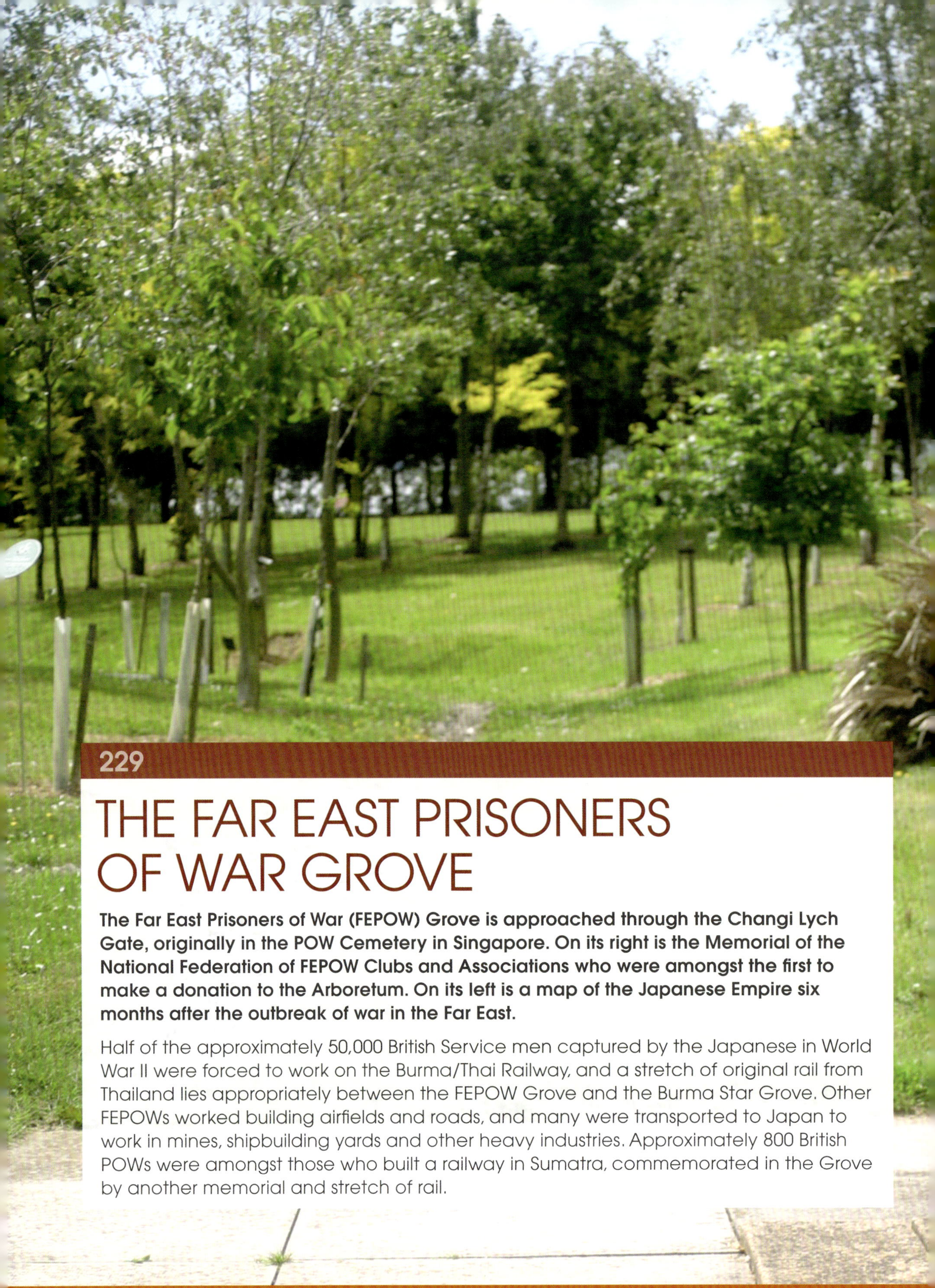

229

# THE FAR EAST PRISONERS OF WAR GROVE

**The Far East Prisoners of War (FEPOW) Grove is approached through the Changi Lych Gate, originally in the POW Cemetery in Singapore. On its right is the Memorial of the National Federation of FEPOW Clubs and Associations who were amongst the first to make a donation to the Arboretum. On its left is a map of the Japanese Empire six months after the outbreak of war in the Far East.**

Half of the approximately 50,000 British Service men captured by the Japanese in World War II were forced to work on the Burma/Thai Railway, and a stretch of original rail from Thailand lies appropriately between the FEPOW Grove and the Burma Star Grove. Other FEPOWs worked building airfields and roads, and many were transported to Japan to work in mines, shipbuilding yards and other heavy industries. Approximately 800 British POWs were amongst those who built a railway in Sumatra, commemorated in the Grove by another memorial and stretch of rail.

Most of the trees in the Grove are dedicated to individual FEPOWs from all three services, and internees. Other trees relate to groups of FEPOWs and four of these are worthy of special mention:

1. The approximately 1,000 UK FEPOWs who died in North Borneo principally on the Death Marches.
2. The approximately 600 UK FEPOWs transported from Singapore who died in or near the Solomon Islands.
3. All FEPOWs lost at sea while being transported.
4. The civilian and military women and children who perished.

Photo by OceanBarefoot

# BURMA RAILWAY

**The memorial has been constructed from 30 metres of the original rails and sleepers used on the Burma Railway which were returned to the Arboretum from Thailand in HMS Northumberland in 2002.**

The memorial is a permanent tribute to those who were forced to construct the infamous 'Railway of Death' and the benches and trees around the railway track have relevant dedications. The memorial was dedicated on 15 August 2002.

231

# THE CHINTHE WOMEN

**The Women's Auxiliary Service (Burma), WAS(B), ran canteens for the Fourteenth Army between 1942 and 1946. They operated close to the frontline, supplying tea, cake and sundries to troops. The Army came to regard them as essential for keeping up troop morale.**

Patricia Wright recalls, "We were all terribly busy manning the static canteen 24 hours a day. We visited units of troops with the mobile canteens as far east as Chiringa and Cox's Bazaar. There were still a lot of enemy troops around."

Pat Wythe gives some details of life in the canteens: "After being kitted out at Shillong, I joined a canteen at Chittagong. We were down at the docks serving 'char and wads' to the troops embarking for the invasion of Ramree Island. We also sold cigarettes, tobacco, razor blades and other shop items."

Betty Donaldson was deeply affected by meeting POWs on their release from the Burma railway. She recounts, "The military had built a shelter and fitted it with tables and chairs. We stood on the runway and watched the small plane glide in. The figures appeared at the doorway and slowly walked down the steps across the dried mud. They all wore some form of hat, most had shoes of a kind, some had a shirt, and if they did not have trousers or shorts they wore a 'jap-happy', a form of nappy tied with string. We led them to the hut and sat them down. Many were stunned to silence. The Army had decided that stew and mashed potatoes, fruit salad and cream was the best meal they could provide. After eating, most of them promptly went to the back of the hut and were sick."

Elaine Cheverton: "We got a reputation for being of value for giving morale and getting stores. It was important that the men could buy their own cigarettes. Chief Commandant Nin Taylor held it together. She was a strong woman and did not take no for an answer. She wanted to go as far forward as possible, but the Divisional Generals were not very happy about having us there."

Mr Pearson: "I had been in Arakan in 1943 and Imphal in 1944 and there were WAS(B) canteens at many of the staging posts up the line from Calcutta. I remember them well. When we were held up at Magwe, two or three of your ladies caught up with us and set up shop near the bank of the Irrawaddy. They made a superb cup of tea in a clean un-chipped mug; the only condition being that you left your hat with them until you brought the mug back. What a delightfully simple system in what was then a very forward area of battle!"

Photo by OceanBarefoot

# ROYAL NORFOLK REGIMENT, SUFFOLK REGIMENT AND CAMBRIDGESHIRE REGIMENT MEMORIAL

**The Royal Norfolk Regiment, originally known as Colonel Cornwall's Regiment of Foot, was the second of eight infantry regiments raised by James II to suppress the Monmouth rebellion in 1685. In 1782 they were accorded the title 9th (East Norfolk) Regiment in recognition of their strong ties with the County of Norfolk. In 1799 HM King George III officially conferred the honour of wearing the figure 'Britannia' as the badge of the Regiment. The 9th was re-titled The Norfolk Regiment and "Rule Britannia" was adopted as the Regimental march in 1881. In June 1935, on the 250th anniversary of the raising of the Regiment, HM King George V bestowed the honour of the prefix 'Royal' in the title of the Regiment.**

The Norfolk Regiment furnished nineteen battalions for war service in World War I and nine in World War II. Five members of the Regiment won the Victoria Cross during World War II, a greater number than any other regiment in the British Army.

In August 1959 the Regiment was amalgamated with the Suffolk Regiment to form the 1st Battn the East Anglian Regiment and in September 1964 became part of the Royal Anglian Regiment.

The Suffolk Regiment was formed in 1685, as The Duke of Norfolk's (12th) Regiment of Foot. The Regiment continued to take the Colonel's name until 1751 when it was designated the 12th of Foot. The links with the county of Suffolk were recognised in 1783 when the Regiment was restyled the 12th (East Suffolk) Regiment. In 1881 the Regiment was re-titled the Suffolk Regiment with two regular and two militia battalions. By 1914 three Territorial Battalions had been added.

During World War I the Regiment expanded to 23 battalions, of which 10 saw active service in France, Gallipoli and the Middle East. Six battalions fought in World War II, including the 7th Battalion which converted to 142nd Regiment RAC, retaining the Suffolk cap badge. The 1st Battalion landed in the leading brigade on D-Day in 1944.

In August 1959 the Regiment was amalgamated with the Royal Norfolk Regiment to form the 1st East Anglian Regiment, which in September 1964 became part of the Royal Anglian Regiment. The 1st Battalion of that Regiment retains links with Suffolk through B (Suffolk) Company.

The volunteer tradition began in 1860 with the Cambridgeshire Rifle Volunteer Corps which was re-titled 3rd (Cambridgeshire) Volunteer Battalion the Suffolk Regiment in 1887. With the formation of the Territorial Force in 1908 the Battalion became 1st Battalion the Cambridgeshire Regiment and saw action in World War I.

The Regiment fought with distinction in Malaya and Singapore until their capitulation in February 1942. The survivors of the two battalions spent the rest of the War as prisoners of the Japanese alongside their comrades in the Royal Norfolk and Suffolk Regiments.

The Regiment reformed in 1947 as 629 (The Cambridgeshire Regiment) Light Anti-Aircraft Regiment RA TA, retaining its cap badge and colours. When the Anti-Aircraft Command was disbanded in 1954 the Regiment reformed once more as 629 (The Cambridgeshire Regiment) Parachute Light Regiment RA TA. In 1956 the Regiment reverted to infantry as the 1st Battalion the Cambridgeshire Regiment, but was amalgamated with 4 Suffolk in 1961 to become 1st Battalion Suffolk and Cambridgeshire Regiment, and was disbanded in 1967.

The 1st Battalion of the Royal Anglian Regiment retains the connection with Cambridgeshire through D (Cambridgeshire) Company.

Photo by David Faul

232

# BURMA STAR

**The Burma Star Association was founded in 1951 for World War II veterans holding the Burma Campaign Star or the Pacific Star with Burma Clasp. The Association's broad aims are to promote the comradeship experienced during those hard times of war and to provide assistance in cases of hardship and distress to veterans, widows and dependants. Some 60 years later the Association still has around 6,000 members worldwide with 100 branches operating in the UK and nine overseas.**

The war in the Far East started in December 1941 simultaneously with the bombing of Pearl Harbour. From early 1942 the Japanese army advanced relentlessly into Burma heading for India. The next three years saw ferocious fighting in the most inhospitable terrain and dense jungle, with extremes of weather further exacerbated by malaria and other tropical diseases. The Fourteenth Army, known to many as 'the Forgotten Army' numbered over one million men under arms, the largest Commonwealth army ever assembled. The Japanese surrendered on 15 August 1945, now known as VJ Day.

The Battle of Kohima was one of the bloodiest battles fought in Burma with the British and Japanese armies fighting in close proximity, separated only by the British Administrator's tennis court.

The memorial here is a smaller replica of the one which stands in the Commonwealth War Cemetery in Kohima and bears the words of the famous Kohima Epitaph which is so poignant to all of those veterans who came home.

"When you go home, tell them of us and say, For your tomorrow, we gave our today."

232a

# THE CHINDIT MEMORIAL

**After the 1942 campaign 77 Brigade was reformed as an airborne force consisting of 1st South Staffords, 1st Kings, 1st Lancashire Fusiliers and 3/6 Ghurkhas, becoming part of 3rd Division.**

Shortly after landing in Burma the Brigade was engaged and successfully defeated a strong Japanese force at Mawlu on the railway north of Mandalay. This first engagement became known as the battle of Pagoda Hill, the fighting was principally hand to hand and there were heavy casualties on both sides. This was where Lieutenant George Cairns, of the Staffords, won the Victoria Cross.

77 Brigade continued to hold Mawlu for two months thus denying supplies by rail to Japanese forces in the Arakan and North Burma, which seriously impaired their campaigns in those areas.

Tragically, the Chindit Force Commander, Major General Orde Wingate, was killed. So was lost an outstanding leader of whom Winston Churchill said "might well have become a man of destiny".

233

# THE IMPERIAL WAR MUSEUM PEACE GARDEN

**Is currently being redesigned.**

234

# THE ROTARY RIDGE

**The hedge of golden Castlewellan cypress that acts as windbreak and backdrop for the Arboretum was first sponsored by local Clubs in Rotary District 1060 as a tribute to the Rotary Clubs in Great Britain and Ireland and Rotary International whose motto is "Service above Self".**

Trees are also dedicated to individual Clubs and Rotarians. Local Rotary Clubs have enthusiastically supported the Arboretum from the early years with individual Rotarians volunteering their skills, business contacts and expertise in many fields.

235

# BRITISH KOREAN VETERANS

**In 1950, 22 member nations of the United Nations (UN) joined South Korean forces to repel the North Korean aggression and stop the spread of Communism. During the three years of the conflict some four million people died. Over 100,000 British Service men served during the war of whom over 2,000 were killed or taken prisoner. Among many decorations awarded were four Victoria Crosses.**

In 1952 the Commonwealth units from Australia, Canada, India, New Zealand and South Africa combined to form the 1st Commonwealth Division.

The Memorial Garden, originally laid out and maintained by members of the British Korean Veterans Association (BKVA), is designed to create a living memorial to all British Service Personnel who served and gave their lives. It is an arboretum within an arboretum planted with more than 100 trees of some 23 different species mostly of Korean or Asian origin.

236

# 17TH DOGRA REGIMENT

**The Dogra Regiment was raised in 1887 from the foothills of the Himalayas and earned laurels for valour in both World Wars, including Nunshigam, Imphal and Kota Bharu in the Second World War Burma campaign. In the pre-independence era, before 1947, the regiment earned three Victoria Crosses and 44 Military Crosses in addition to 312 other awards.**

One of the VCs was awarded to Lance Corporal Naik Lala while serving in Mesopotamia in 1916. He tended and rescued two wounded officers while under heavy shell fire, one of them being Captain Nicholson (later Major General F L Nicholson, CB DSO MC and Colonel of the 1st Battalion from 1934 until 1948), whose name appears on the Regiment's commemorative plaque.

237

# MALAYA & BORNEO VETERANS

**The memorial takes the form of a dagger known as a Kris. The Kris dagger with its wavy blade originates from the Malaya and Borneo region and is associated with jungle and guerrilla warfare.**

Trees dedicated to both regular Service men and National Service men who lost their lives or served during World War II, the Malayan emergency (a state of emergency declared by the British colonial government of Malaya in 1948 and lifted in 1960) and the Borneo confrontation (1962-1966) surround the Kris memorial. Though to all intents and purposes a war, the Malayan emergency was not designated as such in order to avoid the problem of insurance cover for the important rubber plantations.

## 238

# ROYAL MALAYSIAN POLICE

**The memorial is dedicated to all ranks of the former Malayan, Singaporean and Bornean Police Forces, subsequently united in the Royal Malaysian Police. All these forces took part in World War II and subsequent counter-insurgency campaigns fighting alongside Commonwealth military forces between 1948 and 1989.**

In the Malayan Emergency the Royal Malaysian Police suffered 1,300 fatalities.

## 239

# MALAYAN VOLUNTEER FORCE

**The Malayan Volunteers Group, mostly children of volunteers with some veterans, was formed in 2005 to commemorate and raise awareness of the Malayan volunteers in the Malayan Campaign and captivity 1941-1945.**

Some 18,000 volunteers of different races and creeds served in the Malayan Volunteer Forces, Medical Auxiliary Service and Observer Corps, receiving 100 Campaign Awards. In captivity, they contributed practical and medical skills, knowledge of local languages and secret radios, saving lives and giving hope of victory. Others taught in 'Changi University'.

240

# SULTAN OF OMAN'S ARMED FORCES

**The pyramid shaped plinth with its plaque, maps and badge together with four trees of the variety Cypressus sempervirens form a memorial in recognition of all who served in or supported the Armed Forces of the Sultanate of Oman.**

Since their formal establishment in the early 1950s, with British assistance, these forces have twice overcome insurgencies which have threatened the integrity or social structure of the state, and more recently have contributed contingents or facilities to coalitions formed to protect the Persian Gulf states.

They still enjoy a close relationship with the British Military.

241

# BALUCH REGIMENT

**The Regiment was raised in 1820 as a Regiment of Indian Native Infantry and renamed successively The Baluchistan Regiment Bombay Infantry (1895), The Baluchistan Infantry (1902) and The 10th Baluch Regiment (1922).**

They served loyally and in amity under British and Indian officers and fought in campaigns in Abyssinia 1868, China 1900 and in Europe during the First World War 1914–15. Officers who were privileged to lead and serve in the regiment sponsored the grove.

# THE GREEN ZONE

**Access:** Some access from the hard paved Millennium Avenue but most is from 'The Beat' which is a mown grass avenue.

**Terrain:** Firm surface and mown grassland.

**Starting point:** From visitor centre turn right into Millennium Avenue and begin walk from the large gate leading to the car park entrance.

| No | Memorial | Pg |
|---|---|---|
| E | ARMED FORCES MEMORIAL | 7 |
| 301 | NORMANDY VETERANS | 73 |
| 302 | KING'S AFRICAN RIFLES | 73 |
| 303 | THE ROYAL ENGINEERS | 74 |
| 304 | THE FREEMASONS | 74 |
| 305 | THE BEAT (POLICE MEMORIAL AVENUE) | 75 |
| 306 | POLICE MEMORIAL GARDEN | 76 |
| 307 | THE POLAR BEAR MEMORIAL | 76 |

| No | Memorial | Pg |
|---|---|---|
| 308 | BROTHERHOOD OF GREEK VETERANS CHAPEL | 77 |
| 309 | CAVALRY GROVE (CRESCENT) | 77 |
| 310 | THE PHANTOM MEMORIAL | 78 |
| 311 | THE ARMY PARADE | 79 |
| 311a | THE ROYAL GREEN JACKETS | 79 |
| 311b | 10TH ROYAL HUSSARS | 80 |
| 311c | 11TH HUSSARS (THE CHERRY PICKERS) | 80 |
| 312 | WAR WIDOWS' WOOD | 80 |

"I'M GLAD IT WAS RECOGNISED AT LONG LAST – IT'S A LONG TIME AFTER THE WAR."

Veteran Feliks Keidrowski, commented on the Polish Armed Forces Memorial and its recognition of Poland's contribution to the Allied war effort.

THIS MONUMENT WAS
ERECTED BY THE POLISH
EX-COMBATANTS
ASSOCIATION, THE POLISH
AIR FORCE ASSOCIATION
CHARITABLE TRUST,
THE ASSOCIATION
OF THE POLISH KNIGHTS
OF THE SOVEREIGN
MILITARY ORDER
OF MALTA (UK) AND
BY PUBLIC SUBSCRIPTION
THIS MONUMENT
WAS UNVEILED
BY HIS ROYAL HIGHNESS
THE POLISH CAMPAIGN 1939
THE POLISH UNDERGROUND STATE
1939-1945

## 301

# NORMANDY VETERANS

**The Normandy Veterans' memorial was dedicated on 9 August 1999 and became a focus of the 60th Anniversary Commemorations of 6 June 1944 'D' Day Allied Assault, when there was a live video link with the ceremonies attended by HM The Queen in France.**

The avenue of poplar trees, memorial plinth and five stones named for each of the Normandy beaches Utah, Omaha, Gold, Juno and Sword are dedicated to all the men and women who took part in the Normandy Campaign of 1944.

## 302

# KING'S AFRICAN RIFLES

**The King's African Rifles (KAR) started its illustrious career in 1902, battalions being found from Nyasaland, Kenya, Uganda, Tanganyika and later incorporating Northern Rhodesia. Its first major confrontation was in the Tanganyika Campaign fighting the Germans under Vouketow Vorbeck. In 1940 – 1942 battalions were engaged in Evitsea, Abyssinia and Somaliland against the Italians and later in Madagascar. Many battalions moved into Burma from 1944 to the end of fighting there, and after the war were deployed in combatting insurgency in Malaya and Kenya.**

The African soldiers came from a wide variety of tribes and were renowned for their fortitude, good humour and strong sense of discipline. Those lucky enough to have served with them had the privilege of their devoted tenacity and friendship.

The KAR Association has now assumed the duty in providing for the urgent welfare of many old men and widows throughout East Africa.

303

# THE ROYAL ENGINEERS

**The memorial was dedicated in the presence of The Chief Royal Engineer, General Sir Kevin O'Donoghue KCB CBE during a ceremony on 1 May 2007 and commemorates all Royal Engineers ('Sappers') who have fallen in the past and will do so in the future.**

The central features of the monument are four granite rocks each weighing approximately 10 tonnes which were presented to the Corps of Royal Engineers by the people of the Falkland Islands. These four large random blocks of granite present a challenge which is both physical and visual, in bringing them together to form an appropriate and satisfying Memorial. Their weight and mass create an interesting engineering problem which is visually expressed to illustrate the work of the Corps of Royal Engineers. The four stones are placed in a circle and each is raised 150mm above its concrete foundation on a stainless steel dowel, making the huge blocks appear to float above the grass, suggesting a visual metaphor of the ability of the Sapper to intervene in, and control, the physical and geographical environment.

304

# THE FREEMASONS

**The Freemasons' garden is bordered with yew, a symbol of longevity, which surrounds light and dark grey paving reflecting the joys and sorrows of our chequered existence. In addition there are two large stones, one of rough ashlars representing man in his prime and the other polished smooth to represent man in his later years having benefited from education and learning.**

Since the cutting of 'the first sod' on 25 June 2002 the garden is being developed gradually and is designed to include Masonic symbolism that can be readily understood by everyone. The memorial will take decades to reach its true beauty and maturity, but from its earliest stages of construction is a fitting and resilient memorial to past sacrifices and mankind's hopes for the future.

Photo by OceanBarefoot

305

# THE BEAT (POLICE MEMORIAL AVENUE)

**The Beat (Police Memorial Avenue) is planted with a tree for each constabulary in the UK and their badges are represented on plaques beside each tree. Between the constabulary trees are individual dedications. Chestnut was chosen because the first policemen 'peelers' or 'bobbies' carried truncheons made from this wood. The Beat was sponsored by Police Mutual Assurance Society and was opened in September 1996 by the then Home Secretary, Rt Hon Jack Straw MP.**

Each year COPS-UK (Care Of Police Survivors) who look after the families of officers killed in the line of duty, hold a ceremony of Remembrance. All Chief Constables are represented at this moving tribute.

306

# POLICE MEMORIAL GARDEN

**The Police Credit Union sponsored and maintains the memorial garden, designed to be a place of peace and contemplation with its individually dedicated trees, benches and memorial plaques.**

At the entrance to the garden is a memorial chestnut tree grown from a conker collected from the grounds of Drayton Manor Park, the former home of Robert Peel, the founder of the modern police force.

307

# THE POLAR BEAR MEMORIAL

**The Polar Bear Association Memorial was the first monument and sculpture to be placed in the Arboretum. It is a tribute to the 49th Infantry West Riding Division and was dedicated on 7 June 1998. Inheriting the fine reputation forged by its predecessor in World War I, World War II found the 49th Infantry stationed in Iceland and because they were snowed in 20 foot of snow for most of the campaign, their commanding officer called the men 'his Polar Bears'. The Polar Bear on a block of ice was soon adopted as their mascot and shoulder flash.**

Made from yellow hardwood, the bear is 9ft long and 5ft high and weighs 2.5 tonnes; it was created by the Essex Woodcarvers and took a year to carve. Inside the bear is a time capsule containing the names of all the members of the 49th Division who did not come home together with relevant letters and documents.

In the panels set into the brick base of the monument are carvings of the badges of the Regiments of the 49th Infantry with two panels containing the poems written by schoolgirl Jodie Johnson when she was only nine and 11 years of age.

## 308

# BROTHERHOOD OF GREEK VETERANS CHAPEL

**The impressive Greek stone and marble altar in this chapel symbolises the strength of this Brotherhood that was established in April 1991 commemorating the 50th Anniversary of the surrender of The Allied Forces at Kalamata, The Peloponnese and Southern Greece. 10,000 men were captured and became POWs, enduring massive hardship and terrifying trials until Liberation. The horrors of war and incarceration created a band of spirited and brave young men whose camaraderie and resilience survives even to this day.**

The first tree was planted by the Founder and President, Edward Horlington assisted by Reverend Palmer, the son of a Brotherhood Veteran.

### EUROPE 1943 – SECOND ATTEMPTED ESCAPE FROM POW CAMP – FRANK GILL

"Let me tell you, that escaping was no picnic! It indeed was a nerve-wracking, heart-stopping event. The tension was terrible; every movement we heard was treated with suspicion. Every rustle of leaves brought uneasiness. Even your mates' voices, suddenly asking a hushed question caused the blood to flow faster.

Why then, you may ask, bother to break out at all?

Well, adventure and the fact that one's youth was wasting away and one needed to do something to prove that life still held some sort of challenge…

Eventually, after a couple of hours, we emerged from the darkened wood. It was a moonlight night with occasional cloud blackening the sky and shrouding our journey. And as such a night had helped our exploits in crossing the exposed road, so it also became our downfall!"

## 309

# CAVALRY GROVE (CRESCENT)

**This grove consists of a colourful mix of ornamental trees individually dedicated to various Cavalry regiments of the British Army.**

# THE PHANTOM MEMORIAL

**The Phantoms were a wireless communication unit for the Special Air Service (SAS). The Memorial particularly remembers events of 1944 when F Squadron was in France to provide communications for Operation Loyton.**

The path is laid out in a P design to denote the word Phantom. The 140 Rosemary bushes represent the 140 men and boys of Moussey who did not return from concentration camps.

The coral granite memorial stone was cut from a much larger stone at Senone a few miles from Moussey and represents the resolve of the villagers and resistance forces that protected the soldiers on the operation. The Cross of Lorraine was later added to the memorial to represent the Anglo/Norman link.

**Len Owens, who served in the unit and sponsored the memorial has written:**

"Three men of Phantom Signals were killed: two in combat and one man was betrayed, captured, tortured and then killed. 31 men of 2 SAS were killed, the majority killed after capture.

But these losses were small compared with those suffered by the citizens of Moussey and the surrounding area. 220 men and boys were taken to Gestapo HQ and anyone giving information about the SAS was to be allowed to go free. Nobody moved and consequently all were sent to concentration camps named Dachau and Matthausen. Of these 140 did not return. The Mayor of Moussey, Monsieur Jacques Defrance, asked if these 140 could be named on the Phantom Memorial. This was done and also the names of the 31 SAS men who were killed, again mostly after capture. The names of the four British Service women are also given. They were first killed by lethal injection but one recovered and was pushed into the ovens while alive."

# 311

# THE ARMY PARADE

**The Army Parade is laid out in a formal pattern based on the fighting square with dedicated trees, plaques and plinths representing most of the infantry regiments of the British Army.**

# 311a

# THE ROYAL GREEN JACKETS

**On 11 May 2008 over 1,100 former Royal Green Jackets (RGJ) gathered with pride to remember all those who served in the RGJ for the forty years of the Regiment's existence (1966 – 2007) and to dedicate this memorial to them.**

The memorial is of black polished Indian granite and weighs just over two tonnes. It is flanked by Remembrance Trees of the three forming regiments of the RGJ (Oxfordshire, Buckinghamshire Light Infantry, Kings Royal Rifle Corps and Rifle Brigade). A small plaque is placed by the memorial commemorating the dedication event and the unveiling by Field Marshal The Lord Bramall of Bushfield.

The adjacent Armed Forces Memorial has 72 names of RGJ Riflemen and 61 names of the forming regiments of the Royal Green Jackets who were killed on duty or as a result of terrorist action since World War II.

Photo by David Faul

## 311b

# 10TH ROYAL HUSSARS

**At the time of the First Jacobite Rebellion in 1715, the 10th Regiment of Dragoons was raised in Herefordshire by Brigadier Humphrey Gore. The regiment campaigned in the Peninsula War and fought at Waterloo. The 10th were in the Crimea and were awarded two VCs in the South African War.**

In 1784 HM King George III appointed his son, then Prince of Wales, as Colonel of the Regiment which has since borne the title of 'Prince of Wales' Own' with the coronet and feathers, together with the Rising Sun and Red Dragon (an ancient badge of Wales) and the motto "Ich Dien" ("I serve"). In 1806 the Prince of Wales obtained permission to clothe and equip the regiment as Hussars and it thus became the First Hussar Regiment in the British Army. The 10th Royal Hussars has taken part in most of the campaigns of the British Army from the Seven Years War in 1758 to the War of 1939 -1945 and has seen service in most parts of the world. On 25 October 1969 the 10th Royal Hussars (PWO) amalgamated with the 11th Hussars (PAO) to form the Royal Hussars (PWO).

## 311c

# 11TH HUSSARS

### THE CHERRY PICKERS

**The Regiment was formed in 1715. Notable personalities include Lord Cardigan, who led the Regiment in the Charge of the Light Brigade and Prince Albert (husband of Queen Victoria) from whom the Regiment got its famous cherry coloured trousers. The nickname Cherrypickers came after an action in a cherry orchard.**

In World War II, the Regiment led the Desert Rats, the 7th Armoured Division, and were the first British troops into Berlin. The 77 battle honours shown on the memorial tell the full story. The Regiment was amalgamated with the 10th Royal Hussars in 1969.

## 312

# WAR WIDOWS' WOOD

**This planting is a mixture of individually dedicated native trees sponsored by war widows in memory of their husbands who never returned from conflict.**

313

# MEDITERRANEAN CAMPAIGNS OF THE SECOND WORLD WAR

**The Mediterranean Garden is laid out geographically with, at the far side, the outline of the North African coast. Here trees native to that region have been planted to commemorate those who served with the 1st and 8th Armies. There is also a stone memorial to the famous Rats of Tobruk who endured one of the longest sieges in British and Commonwealth military history. Another stone plinth recalls those who served in Palestine before Israel gained independence. On the near side the garden, in the shape of Sicily and Italy, has been planted with Black Pine, each tree linked to one of the major battles of the Italian Campaign. Other memorials and trees in this plot are relevant to the Mediterranean Campaigns. The Siege of Malta 1940–1943 is commemorated by a brick built, shrub-planted Cross of St John.**

## GEORGE CROSS ISLAND ASSOCIATION

**Malta, a small island in the Eastern Mediterranean, has been of strategic importance for thousands of years. Phoenicians, Greeks, Romans, Byzantines, Turks and Knights of St John have either governed it or fought for it. The British won it from the French during the Napoleonic Wars at the request of the Maltese people and, after becoming independent from Britain in 1964, Malta became a Republic in 1974.**

Malta's role in World War II was crucial in order to maintain supply lines through the Mediterranean. Germany and Italy were determined to bombard and starve its defenders and inhabitants into submission. Bombing raids were continuous and heavy, particularly during 1941/2 with nearly 3,000 raids. During a six-week period in 1942, a total of 6,700 tons of bombs fell around Grand Harbour alone. This compares with 250 tons when Coventry suffered its own blitz. Despite the efforts of the allied convoys, many of which were sunk, food was scarce and severely rationed. In 1942 surrender was almost inevitable with only 10 days of supplies left but the Maltese were determined not to give in. Survival was assured with the arrival of the Pedestal Convoy in August 1942, an event which continues to be commemorated annually both in Malta and the UK. The islanders of Malta were awarded the George Cross by King George VI in recognition of their "heroism and devotion" and numerous service personnel also received medals.

The George Cross Island Association (GCIA) was founded in 1987 by Fred Plenty, formerly of the Royal Navy, with the main aim of "Honouring the people of Malta and those who fought on their behalf by reuniting members in a unique bond of friendship". Many GCIA members and families in the UK, Malta and overseas subscribed to the Malta garden at the Arboretum as their own tribute, and they continue to meet for reunions in Malta and throughout Britain.

## THE PALESTINE POLICE OLD COMRADES' ASSOCIATION

**The Palestine Police Old Comrades' (PPOC) Association was formed after the termination of the British Mandate of Palestine on 15 May 1948. The Force had been in existence since 1 July 1920 during which time over 500 personnel had been lost, of which 353 were British, to terrorist activities which occurred throughout the period of the Mandate. The Association still exists and circulates a newsletter to approximately 700 members over 60 years after 'The Force' ceased to exist.**

A contingent went to HABFORCE (Iraq 1941) and the Syrian campaign, and it had a Port & Marine Section under Admiralty Fleet Orders, wearing naval uniforms. King George VI held an inspection of a contingent of 'The Force' at Buckingham Palace on 20 July 1948 during which he presented various medals in recognition of gallantry and meritorious service.

## THE PALESTINE VETERANS ASSOCIATION

**The Palestine Veterans Association (PVA) represents the 90,000 British troops who were sent to Palestine to deal with the situation which had arisen there after World War II. Having survived the Holocaust, the displaced Jews in Europe were desperate to reach "The Promised Land". The quota for immigrants was pitifully low, consequently vast numbers tried to gain access in ships which were hardly seaworthy.**

There were 784 service fatalities together with 400 members of the Palestine Police killed in the line of duty. Apart from Korea this was, and remains, the highest loss of life in any conflict since 1945. A statement explaining the feelings of personnel at the time was common, "For those at home the war is over, for us it has just begun."

313a

# THE ARMY WOOD

**The Army Wood consists of mixed native trees individually sponsored and dedicated to those who have served in the British Armed Forces.**

314

# ROYAL LOGISTIC CORPS

**The grove, including the memorial plinth and surrounding edible wild plants such as bramble, crab apple, hawthorn and rose, was dedicated on 11 September 2000 as a tribute to The Royal Logistic Corps. Since the formation of the Corps in 1993, it has been their responsibility to sustain British Armed forces wherever they are deployed.**

During the periods of tension, wars and peacekeeping operations, members of the Corps have been awarded the George Cross and George Medal, and in the case of the late Warrant Officer 2 (WO2) O'Donnell, a bar to his George Medal.

The RLC serves at sea and in the air, as well as carrying out a number of significant and technical roles on land. The RLC's mission is to "Fight Logistics through" and it delivers whatever the cost.

## ARMY TRAINING REGIMENT (ATR) BASSINGBOURN

**Bassingbourn in Cambridgeshire began its proud association with the British Armed Forces when the RAF built a camp there in 1934. During World War II the barracks were run by the United States Army Air Forces (USAAF) with the famous Memphis Belle, as well as many less famous aircraft, conducting bombing missions across Europe. The camp was returned to the RAF after the war and handed on to the British Armed Forces in 1969.**

Bassingbourn Barracks is now home to an Army Training Regiment where civilians are transformed into basic soldiers ready for Special to Army Training in the Household Cavalry, Royal Armoured Corps, Royal Engineers and Royal Electrical and Mechanical Engineers.

315

# KENYA POLICE

**The bench, tree and plaques were dedicated on 20 October 2004 to remember all ranks who served in the Kenya Police and Kenya Police Reserve up to the year 1963, when Kenya was granted independence from Britain.**

316

# ROYAL MILITARY POLICE ASSOCIATION

**The plinth, flagpole and carved wooden bench of the Royal Military Police Association (RMPA) memorial are dedicated to the men and women of the Military Police who have given their lives in the service of their country. Their motto is "Exemplo Ducemus", "by example we lead".**

The Royal Military Police (RED CAPS) memorial shows the figure of a RMP which was brought to the Arboretum from the old barracks in Chichester and is known as 'FOXY' after Corporal Fox, the model.

A common punishment at the barracks for bad behaviour was to clean the brass plaque on the side of the figure.

317

# SOROPTIMIST INTERNATIONAL

**Soroptimist International, a worldwide organisation for women in management and the professions, is a global voice for women through awareness, advocacy and action.**

Soroptimist International is a vibrant, dynamic organisation for today's professional and business women. They are committed to a world where women and girls together achieve their individual and collective potential, realise aspirations and have an equal voice in creating strong, peaceful communities worldwide.

The name Soroptimist derives from the Latin soror, meaning sister and optima, meaning best. It is best translated as 'best of sisters'.

318

# BRITISH GERMAN FRIENDSHIP GARDEN

**This thoughtfully designed peace grove was officially inaugurated by the Duke of Kent in October 2006 to celebrate 60 years of peace and reconciliation between the United Kingdom and Germany.**

The garden design has two circles of silver birch and a circle of stones retrieved from the rubble of the Frauenkirche in Dresden which was destroyed by Allied bombing during World War II. Each of the smoke blackened stones displays a plaque bearing the name of a German or British city that suffered heavy damage during the conflict. In the centre of the garden is the Dresden Oak, gifted by the Dresden Trust and nearby stands a Gingko (recalling Goethe's poem) and two trees presented by one-time enemy combatants.

319

# ANGLO-JAPANESE PEACE GROVE

**The Anglo-Japanese Peace Grove was dedicated jointly by the Japanese Ambassador and Mrs. Keiko Holmes on 15 August 2001. Mrs Holmes is the founder president of Agape, the organisation working for reconciliation between Far East Prisoners of War (FEPOWs), their families and the Japanese.**

The Stone of Reconciliation stands amongst a planting of European and Japanese maples whose brightly coloured leaves will intermingle as they fall in autumn, symbolising friendship between nations that were once bitter enemies. The flowering cherry trees in the adjoining grove were individually sponsored by Japanese businesses and families.

320

# CELEBRATION OF LIFE GROVE

**Supported by the Midlands Co-operative Society the grove is a large semi-circular planting of mixed spring flowering blossom trees individually dedicated as a celebration of the life of family members and friends who have passed away.**

321

# IRAQ/AFGHANISTAN WILLOWS

**This planting is a sweeping avenue of weeping willows alongside the Darbyshire Ditch, which are individually sponsored and dedicated to servicemen and women who have lost their lives in Iraq and Afghanistan.**

321a

# BASRA MEMORIAL WALL

**The Basra Memorial Wall is a truly poignant monument to the 178 UK Service personnel and one Ministry of Defence (MoD) civilian who lost their lives on combat operations in Iraq and also lists members of Coalition Forces who were killed whilst under UK command during six years of conflict.**

The original memorial was built in Basra in 2006 and stood outside the front of the Headquarters of the Multi-National Division (South East). Following the end of operations, the Basra Memorial Wall was brought back to the UK and rebuilt. The original wall was built and dismantled, and the new wall constructed at the Arboretum by British soldiers from 37th Armoured Engineer Squadron in a personal gesture to commemorate their fallen comrades.

The brass plaques on this memorial are the originals placed on the wall when it was in situ in Basra, Iraq. The plaques are cleaned twice a year; before the anniversary of the end of combat operations in Iraq and before Armistice, but in between they will be allowed to weather naturally. This will allow the detail on these original plaques to last for as long as possible for the benefit of future generations.

322

# THE NAVY WOOD

**The Navy Wood consists of mixed native trees individually sponsored and dedicated to those who have served in the British Royal Navy and Merchant Navy.**

323

# THE BLUES AND ROYALS

**The curved avenue of blue and gold conifers, bench and memorial plinth of Derbyshire limestone and polished granite are dedicated to the memory of all ranks of The Royal Horse Guards, The Royal Dragoons and the Blues and Royals who have died whilst in the service of their country at home and overseas from 1945 to the present day.**

The Derbyshire limestone memorial stone from Longcliffe Quarries Limited of Matlock was donated by Mr Robert Shields, a former High Sheriff of Derbyshire.

324

# ROYAL TANK REGIMENT

**The very first battle involving tanks took place on the Somme when approximately 30 tanks attacked German positions between the villages of Flers and Courcelette on Friday 15 September 1916. This was one of the largest battles of World War I, with more than one million casualties. At dawn on 20 November 1917 the first successful tank battle was fought at Cambrai involving some 300 Mark IV tanks. The arrival of the tank signalled the end of trench warfare and established the tank as a dominant factor of battle right up to the present day.**

The design of the Royal Tank Regiment grove reflects these events with a collection of Ash trees, a tree of significance to the Regiment, some of which have been propagated from trees from the battlefield at Cambrai while inside the circular seat is an oak tree from Flers. On the brick plinth is a model of a Mark IV, one of the earliest tanks. In the spring the Grove bursts into colour with hundreds of daffodils planted in the pattern of tank tracks. On the flagpole flies the Regimental flag of brown, red and green signifying 'through mud and blood to green fields beyond.'

325

# MERCIAN WOOD

**This is a small mixed species woodland of individually dedicated trees.**

325a

# ROYAL CORPS OF SIGNALS

**The Royal Signals Association (RSA) was formed in 1920 as the 'Royal Engineers Old Comrades Association Signals Branch'. The Association aims to provide comfort and relief to past and present signallers and their dependants who are in conditions of need, hardship or distress. It also exists to foster comradeship and morale within the Corps family, serving and retired. The RSA has 68 branches in the UK and 28 Unit Associations that are affiliated.**

The Corps Memorial was unveiled by the Colonel in Chief, The Princess Royal, in May 2008. This is a statue depicting the cap badge of the Royal Corps of Signals which represents Mercury, messenger to the Gods. It has been given the nickname 'Jimmy' by the Corps.

No-one is certain how this nickname came about, one theory being that the figure is based upon a sculpture by Giambologna, an Italian, whose name was eventually shortened to Jimmy. More likely is that it followed the popularity of a member of the Corps Jimmy Emblem, who was the British Army boxing champion in 1926!

326

# IRISH INFANTRY GROVE

**In June 2000, Archbishop Robin Eames of Armagh and many hundreds of members of the Irish Infantry Regiments gathered to dedicate this plot which is planted with trees native to Ireland. The grove includes Irish yews and an oak from a stand of oak in Tollymore Forest Park which was one of the few species in Ireland to have survived the last Ice Age.**

The grove with its memorial stone of Belfast black and Mourne granites commemorates all the members of the Irish Infantry Regiments who have served the Crown since the raising of the original Royal Irish Regiment (18th) in 1684.

327

# THE GOLDEN GROVE

**This raised circular earthwork contains a planting of dedicated golden trees and shrubs to celebrate the lives of couples of the World War II generation who have been married for 50 years.**

The taller trees of the innermost ring are golden stemmed ash and these are surrounded by Malus and Sorbus that bear golden fruit. The first tree in this grove was planted by HRH the Duke of Kent to celebrate the Golden Wedding Anniversary of HM The Queen and Prince Phillip. In the autumn of 1999 the Staffordshire Guides planted over 10,000 daffodil bulbs on the inside bank of the Golden Grove as their Millennium Project making a glorious show each Spring.

327a

Photo: copyright National Memorial Arboretum

# POLISH FORCES WAR MEMORIAL

**The memorial commemorates the Polish men and women who gave their lives in World War II. Polish Armed Forces veterans from across the UK joined guests including HRH The Duke of Kent, Her Excellency Barbara Krystyna Tuge-Erecińska, Ambassador of the Republic of Poland, senior figures from the UK and Polish governments and their Armed Forces, to dedicate the memorial on 10 September 2009.**

The memorial is superbly located at the eastern end of The Beat. Four humble toy soldiers, each painted a bronze colour and glued back-to-back atop a two-penny piece provided the inspiration behind the memorial's design. The statue is set within an 18 metre diameter architectural feature which has a series of inset plaques describing the Polish contribution in World War II. The memorial was made in Poland – the four figures represent their army, navy, air force and underground movement. Incorporated within the statue is the symbol of the Polish Eagle (the Polish State emblem), uniting all four sculptures under its outspread wings. The feature was designed by London-based civil engineering and architectural services company, Soarbond Ltd.

During World War II the Polish were the fourth largest fighting force on the Allied side. They were also instrumental in helping the Allies to crack the Enigma code as explained on the plaque on the wall. Even before 1939 there were two Poles working on the code and the underground fighters made sure all their notes came to Britain.

The memorial is designed to act not only as a tribute to the fallen, but also as an educational aid for those visitors not familiar with the history of the Allied Polish Forces.

Photo by OceanBarefoot

## 328

# ROYAL ARMY MEDICAL CORPS

**This large woodland has red and gold leaved trees individually dedicated to members of the Royal Army Medical Corps (RAMC).**

A memorial plinth stands at the entrance to a central avenue of purple leaved trees planted as a tribute to the 29 members who were awarded the Victoria Cross, two of them gaining the award twice. HM Queen Elizabeth The Queen Mother was Colonel in Chief of the Corps and the RAMC planted a tree in the grove to commemorate her 100th birthday.

## 329

# SHOT AT DAWN

**During World War I some 306 British and Commonwealth soldiers were shot for desertion or cowardice. Most of them were sentenced after a short trial at which no real opportunity for defence was allowed. Today, it is recognised that several of them were under age when they volunteered and that many of them were suffering from shell shock or post traumatic stress disorder.**

Andy Decomyn's statue 'Shot at Dawn' is modelled on Private Herbert Burden, of the 1st Battalion Northumberland Fusiliers, who was shot at Ypres in 1915, aged 17.

The names of Herbert Burden and those others who suffered the fate of being shot at dawn are listed on the stakes arranged in the form of a Greek theatre around the statue, symbolising the tragedy that these events signify. Many of the posts say 'Age Unknown' and this is because many young men lied about their age in order to enlist. Some of them had no representation at court-martial because most of the officers had been killed when they went 'over the top' first. (The average life expectancy of an officer on the front line was 10 weeks).

We know of these 306 soldiers, but we do not know the total figure because between 80% and 90% of those sentenced to die had their sentences commuted and were probably sent to jail or hard labour.

Many visitors ask about the location of the memorial in the Arboretum. It seems appropriate that it should be on the eastern edge where dawn strikes first.

The six trees facing the posts represent the firing squad, all aiming for the medallion around the statue's neck and none of them knowing who had the fatal bullet. It must have been very traumatic for them too, having to shoot one of their own.

Photo by OceanBarefoot

## THE CAMPAIGN FOR A PARDON:

**After the 75 year Secrecy Act was lifted, members of the Shot at Dawn Organisation started campaigning for pardons.**

The campaign commenced in 1992 and was led by Janet Booth who sought a pardon for her Grandfather, Private Harry Farr. Janet's grandmother had lived with the shame and stigma of her husband being shot for cowardice in 1916. She believed he was wrongly convicted and actually suffered from 'shellshock'. Harry Farr's family took the Ministry of Defence to the High Court and won. In 2006 a posthumous pardon was granted for Harry and the other men.

330

# LICHFIELD WOOD

**The City of Lichfield Wood was sponsored by the Swinfen Broun Trust, a local charity.**

The mix of native trees includes species relating to districts of the city such as The Cherry Orchard. The name Lichfield derives from an early English phrase meaning 'the clearing in the grey woods' and some of the trees here are native ones with grey bark. Many of the trees have been sponsored by local groups and individuals associated with or living in the Lichfield District area.

Photo by OceanBarefoot

330a

# THE SHOWMEN'S GUILD OF GREAT BRITAIN

**This unique memorial commemorates members of the Guild who have died during conflict. The Showmen's Guild of Great Britain is the trade association for the travelling funfair industry. It represents the 4,100 members who operate the majority of travelling funfairs throughout Great Britain and Northern Ireland. The 23,500 family members between them run over 100 fairs weekly throughout the year.**

The Showmen's Guild members are, through their work in running fairs, responsible for raising thousands of pounds for local, regional and national charities.

James Albert Ryan, Showman from the Midland Section was the original 'Private Ryan' from Walsall, whose experiences were the inspiration for the Tom Hanks / Stephen Spielberg 1998 Hollywood blockbuster. In reality, James was in the Tank Division of 30 Corps working on the dangerous task of mine clearance.

George Thompson, Showman from Blackpool served in the D-Day Landings with HMS Dispatch and subsequently saw action across Europe including in France, the German Rhine and defending Holland's tidal dykes. Additionally, he was among those sent to relieve the victims of Auschwitz in Poland.

331

# KINGFISHER WOOD

**A mixed woodland of individually dedicated native trees named after the kingfishers seen flying along the nearby river bank.**

331a

# ARMY APPRENTICE NATIONAL MEMORIAL

**To be dedicated in September 2011.**

332

Photo by OceanBarefoot

# HOUSEHOLD DIVISION

**On top of the stone plinth stands a copy of the railings from the old Chelsea barracks, and mounted onto them are the original five Garter stars and badges of the foot guards. On the rear of the plinth are the mottos of the five Regiments of Foot Guards in the Household Division.**

**Welsh:** "Wales for ever"

**Irish:** "Who shall separate us"

**Coldstream:** "Second to none"

**Grenadiers:** "Evil be to him who evil thinks"

**Scots:** "No one assails me with impunity"

The badges of the Household Cavalry are in the most senior positions on the memorial, out on the flanks, while the guards are placed in order of seniority, with the Grenadier Guards on the right flank then the Scots Guards, the Welsh Guards and the Irish Guards with the Coldstream Guards on the left. These positions are as the Guards would have been placed facing the enemy, so look to be in reverse order when seen from the front.

The memorial is paved with coloured stones interlocking with each other. These stones have been taken from England (white granite), Scotland (red granite), Ireland (green limestone) and Wales (black slate). The stones represent the union of the regiments despite their rivalry.

Around the back of the memorial are five Wellingtonia trees, also known as Giant redwood or Giant sequoia. These trees were chosen because the Duke of Wellington had connections with The Guards during the Napoleonic Wars.

The years shown are those in which each regiment swore allegiance to the British Crown although some were originally founded before that date.

## 332a

# ROYAL ELECTRICAL AND MECHANICAL ENGINEERS

**The two badges at the side of the seat are their old badge and their new one. Future planting includes oak trees and bluebells; 'bluebell' was the Royal Electrical and Mechanical Engineers (REME) call sign.**

The small memorial to the right remembers a soldier from REME who was killed in Bosnia. It originally marked the spot in Bosnia where he died, but was brought back to the UK when troops pulled out.

## 333

# ROYAL AIR FORCE WOOD

**This is a woodland of mixed native trees alongside the River Tame dedicated to individuals who have served in the Royal Air Force.**

## 332b

# LIGHT INFANTRY MEMORIAL

**This Portland stone monolith and adjacent benches, dedicated on 12 June 2011, are "In proud memory of all those who served in the Light Infantry". The eight Regiments whose names are carved on the seats all served as Light Infantry after the formation of the Light Infantry Group in 1946 although they were all granted the honour of the title Light Infantry in the 19th Century.**

At one time the Light Infantry was the largest regiment of infantry in the British Army. In 2007 the Light Infantry became a constituent part, with the Royal Green Jackets and two other distinguished Regiments, of a new, large regiment The Rifles. They proudly retain the Bugle cap badge which features on the stone – the universal symbol of the founder regiments.

334

# ROYAL AIR FORCE CRANWELL APPRENTICES

**A Staffordshire blue brick plinth and memorial plaque, sponsored by the Royal Air Force Cranwell Apprentices Association in 2005, is dedicated to all aircraft apprentices who trained at Royal Air Force Cranwell from 1922 to 1952. Cranwell is currently the home of the Royal Air Force College.**

335

# ROYAL AIR FORCE BOY ENTRANTS

**The RAF Boy Entrants memorial was dedicated on 11 September 2004 in memory of the many thousands of Boy Entrants who trained between 1934 and 1965 and to record their singular contribution to the Royal Air Force.**

The memorial design includes a stone monolith carved by Viv Astling, sculptor and stone mason who located the piece of 'Ancaster' hard white stone. The names of the 10 RAF Stations where Boy Entrants trained are mounted on the Staffordshire blue brick plinths.

336

# COASTAL COMMAND

**Founded on 14 July 1936, Coastal Command with its motto "Constant Endeavour" was an organisation within the Royal Air Force which defended the United Kingdom from Naval threats and countered German U-Boats from the air.**

The memorial grove of the maritime variety of Corsican pine trees is dedicated to all who served in Coastal Command and Flying Boats, and is appropriately situated overlooking the water of the River Tame.

## COASTAL FORCES VETERANS' ASSOCIATION

**In 1974 the Coastal Forces Veterans' Association was formed by crews of the 'Little Ships'; Motor Torpedo Boats (MTBs), Motor Gun Boats and Motor Launches, who served in the Royal Navy from 1939 to 1957. Their motto is "To upkeep the spirit of comradeship that prevailed in the boats".**

The boats took the war to the enemy, attacking ships at short range, laying and sweeping mines, defending convoys, carrying out air-sea rescue and supporting the major landings at Dunkirk, Dieppe, Sicily, Salerno and Normandy. They played a major role in the success of the St Nazaire attack, losing 14 out of 17 Motor Launches. Many decorations were awarded to officers and men, bearing witness to their gallantry and spirit.

## 337

# ROYAL NATIONAL LIFEBOAT INSTITUTION

**This memorial has been designed to reflect the work of Royal National Lifeboat Institution (RNLI) crews and the relationship between crew members, a rescued person and all their families whose lives become interwoven during a rescue. It is intended not only as a celebration and recognition of the work of the RNLI but also to honour those crew members and people who have lost their lives saving others.**

The design was created by gardener and TV presenter Chris Beardshaw and is an enhancement of the original memorial that was designed and funded by local volunteers.

Chris Beardshaw has created a coastal scene – a beautiful space in which to contemplate and reflect on the work of the RNLI. It embodies the journey of one member of a volunteer crew. As you enter you'll see the statue of a lifeboat crew member, created by Andrew Fitchett. Take the path going to the left, and the colours of the plants are calm and muted like the sea on a calm day. The stone monoliths represent more crew members heading out on a rescue mission. As you pass by the groynes and beach, you overlook the water. The colours change to shades of red to embody danger and stormy waters. The stone cairn represents those rescued encircled by the crew and the last stone monolith on your journey symbolizes the crews and survivors returning to safety and their families.

The memorial's aim is to encourage the visitor to reflect on the sacrifice given by those crew members who did not return.

## 337a

# SHACKLETON ASSOCIATION MEMORIAL

**The Avro Shackleton was in service with the RAF and the South African AF from 1951 to 1991. Known by many as the work horse of the Cold War they were used in anti-submarine, maritime reconnaissance, air sea rescue and airborne early warning roles. During those forty years, 16 aircraft were lost with 150 fatalities. Patrols of fourteen hours were not uncommon, which stretched the endurance of the aircrews and the skill of the ground crews in keeping them airworthy.**

The memorial was erected by the Shackleton Association and is dedicated to all who served with Shackleton squadrons and units.

Photo by OceanBarefoot

338

# THE 41 CLUB

**The 41 Club is an association of past members of the Round Table – The National Association of Round Tables in Great Britain and Ireland.**

Round Table was founded by Louis Marchesi, a Rotarian, in Norwich in 1927, for young men aged between 18 and 40. He was inspired by a speech by the then Prince of Wales who said "The young business and professional men of this country must get together round the table, adopt methods that have proved so sound in the past, adapt them to the changing needs of the times and wherever possible, improve them".

This memorial celebrates the community service achievements and the millions of pounds raised for charities by Round Tablers since then. It takes the form of a garden with 41 trees, surrounding an obelisk.

Originally Round Tablers had to retire at 40 (hence the name 41 Club), but in 1988 the age limit was raised to 45. This Garden was created by Lichfield 41 Club, following a national appeal to the Association of Ex-Round Tablers' Clubs – 41 Club.

339

# ANCIENT BURIAL MOUND

**This is a 3,000 year old Bronze Age Burial Mound and because it is classed as a scheduled ancient monument cannot be planted with trees or built upon. The mound has not been quarried and is being developed as a wildflower meadow providing a haven for wildlife.**

340

# THE ROYAL OBSERVER CORPS

**The Observer Corps founded in 1925 to track aircraft was a uniformed volunteer organisation that enjoyed a long association with the Royal Air Force. The badge of the Royal Observer Corps depicts a beacon lighter of Elizabethan times and the Corps motto "Forewarned is Forearmed".**

The Observer Corps was one of the cornerstones of Lord Dowding's air defence system during World War II. In 1941 HM King George VI conferred the title 'Royal' for the sterling service given by the Observer Corps during the Battle of Britain and in September of that year women were enrolled in the Corps. In 1944 some 796 members of the Observer Corps volunteered to man the Defensively Equipped Merchant Ships during the D-Day Landings. These volunteers were temporarily seconded to the Royal Navy in the rank of Petty Officer/ Aircraft Identifier and wore 'Seaborne' flashes on their uniform. Three members lost their lives on board.

During the Cold War the Corps was given a nuclear reporting role, passing information to Military and Civil Authorities. In 1991 the reduced nuclear threat to the United Kingdom resulted in the stand-down of the majority of volunteer members of the Royal Observer Corps. In 1995, the decision was finally taken to stand-down the remaining elements of the Corps, completing 70 years of outstanding voluntary service at the forefront of the defence of the realm. The Royal Observer Corps Association was formed in 1986 to bring together former members of the Royal Observer Corps and to keep them in touch with each other.

340a

# ROYAL AIR FORCE ASSOCIATION REMEMBRANCE GARDEN

**The first national Remembrance garden in memory of all those who have served in the RAF and Commonwealth air forces was opened by HRH The Princess Royal on Monday 28 September 2009.**

The inspiration for the Remembrance garden comes from the RAF Association's Dedication, the last line of which is "we will remember them". The central feature of the 50 metre-long garden is the RAF Association emblem – a magnificent stainless steel eagle sitting on top of a globe. The eagle, named Winston, is made up of over 1,000 hand-forged feathers and is surrounded by a segmented RAF roundel separated into four quarters to depict the RAF Association at the heart of RAF welfare.

The RAF Association provides friendship, help and support for any members of the RAF past and present, and their families. It is also the largest single-service membership organisation in the United Kingdom, with around 74,000 members and almost 500 branches.

The RAF Association Remembrance Garden will preserve the memory of serving and ex-serving members of the RAF for many years to come. Relatives, friends and colleagues of anyone who has served in the RAF will be able to create a permanent memorial by planting an individual cross in the garden in memory of their loved one. For more information on this process, please visit www.rafa.org.uk.

Royal Air Forces Association

341

# ROYAL & SUN ALLIANCE MEMORIALS

**Two large carved memorials complete the collection of memorial plaques displayed on the wooden walls of the Cloister Walk.**

The memorials are from insurance companies that have amalgamated with other companies and moved to new premises. These elegant memorials remember members of their staff who served and fell during the two World Wars.

341a

# NO 30 SQUADRON ASSOCIATION

**On 10 September 2008, No 30 Squadron Association dedicated the first memorial at the Arboretum to a current flying Squadron. No 30 Squadron Association was formed in 1985 under the Chairmanship of Air Vice Marshal David Dick, who had served on Thunderbolts in Burma. He was also the test pilot who intentionally put the Javelin aircraft into a spin to explore why it happens and to find a procedure to help pilots recover from a spin.**

From its formation in Egypt in 1915 to its present role as part of the Lyneham Transport Wing, No 30 Squadron has always justified its motto "Ventre a Terr", translated as "Flat Out". The Squadron pioneered the dropping of supplies to beleaguered troops in Mesopotamia in World War I and was instrumental in devising an aerial policing policy during the inter-war period. In Greece during World War II, 30 Squadron's Blenheims took part in many raids on the advancing enemy before being forced to retreat. After re-grouping the Squadron served in Ceylon (now Sri Lanka) and India and, during the latter stages of the war, in a fighter-bomber role in Burma. In the late 1940s, the Squadron took on its present role of air transportation, participating in the Berlin Airlift and progressing from Dakotas through Valettas and Beverleys to its present aircraft, the C130 Hercules; first the 'K' model and now the Hercules 'J'. The Hercules has flown in all recent major operations including the Falklands, the Gulf Wars, the Balkans, Iraq, and now in Afghanistan. Every Humanitarian Relief Operation around the world has seen 30 Squadron crews participating. The Squadron's Battle Honours are engraved on the reverse side of the memorial.

No 30 Squadron and its Association have a very close bond and the membership is still in excess of 300 with many wartime veterans. The stories they tell sound much the same as those told by the young aircrew who have flown the Hercules 'J' model in Iraq and Afghanistan.

342

# ROYAL AIR FORCE SERVICING COMMANDO AND TACTICAL SUPPLY WING ASSOCIATION

**The avenue of 16 maple trees, dedicated bench and memorial plinth is a tribute to the RAF Servicing Commandos.**

In January 1942 a memo signed by Louis Mountbatten was sent from War Cabinet Annex to the Air Ministry proposing the formation of RAF Servicing Commandos. World War II Commando Units were trained along similar lines to the Army and Royal Marine Commandos, supervised by the Army. Training was followed by amphibious exercises at the Combined Training Centre at Inveraray.

Units operated in Normandy and the Continent, India, Burma, Indo-China (Saigon) and Java, North Africa, Sicily and Italy.

343

# ROYAL AUXILIARY AIR FORCE

**The impressive brick memorial topped with a large antique metal cast of an eagle is to commemorate all who served in the Royal Auxiliary Air Force (RAuxAF).**

The memorial and surrounding trees were dedicated in September 2004 by HRH the Duke of Gloucester. The RAuxAF was formed in 1924 to provide a reserve of part-time volunteers who could be called upon to support the RAF during times of need. The squadrons served with distinction during World War II, especially during the Battle of Britain, were re-formed in 1946 and largely disbanded in 1957 but have since been revived with some 20 units currently in existence.

## 343a

# AIRCREW ASSOCIATION MEMORIAL

**The memorial consists of a Mountsorrell red granite rough hewn stone displaying the propeller logo.**

The Aircrew Association was founded on 8 September 1977 to foster comradeship amongst aircrew who had been awarded a military flying badge.

## 344

# ROYAL AIR FORCE WING

**The RAF memorial grove (RAF Wing) comprises a collection of silver birch trees planted in the shape of an eagle's wings. One wing is in honour of Fighter Command and the other Bomber Command. The trees are individually dedicated to some of the Squadrons. The central 'three bladed propeller' made up of dwarf golden honeysuckle plants was sponsored by the Aircrew Association.**

## 344a

# THE ROYAL AIR FORCE POLICE

**The Royal Air Force (RAF) Police have been supporting worldwide RAF operations since 1918. Peaking in 1945, the branch comprised 20,500 personnel and by 1948 RAF Police investigators had brought to justice the surviving killers of 50 RAF officers who had taken part in the Great Escape.**

HM King George VI approved the RAF Police badge & motto in 1950 and throughout the 30 year 'Cold War' the branch provided security protection for the RAF's nuclear deterrent. Having served in 66 countries since 1918, the RAF Police are today in the forefront of the war against terrorism serving in current conflicts. The RAF Police Association was formed in 1984. The RAF nickname for their police is 'Snowdrops' because they wear white hats, and this is reflected in the flowers engraved on the edges of the stone.

345

# WOMEN'S AUXILIARY AIR FORCE

**The Women's Auxiliary Air Force (WAAF) memorial represents their badge with the King's Crown emblem.**

The cut-out letters on the upper roundel record all the important roles that the young women carried out between 1939 and 1945. The light passes through these words onto the plinth below and are seen as 'shadows of remembrance' in memory of those who lost their lives.

346

# AIR FORMATION AND AIR SUPPORT SIGNALS

**By the end of World War II, some 21,000 soldiers, predominantly members of the Royal Corps of Signals, provided communications for Royal Air Force bases overseas.**

The crescent of ten copper beech trees remembers soldiers who have provided communications for the Royal Air Force from October 1917 to the present day. In all military operations and natural disasters they are among the vanguard, first in and last out. Three detachments landed in Normandy on D-Day and at present they provide communications for the Joint Helicopter Force in Afghanistan.

## 346a

# 90 SIGNALS UNIT

**90 Signals Unit (90SU) provides a vital role in ensuring the RAF achieves operational success and exists to provide Expeditionary Information Services, whenever they are required.**

Comprising two Wings, Force Generation Wing (FGW) and Tactical Communications Wing (TCW), the Unit's history can be traced back to the mid 1950s, although TCW did not become an autonomous signals unit until later (1973). Since this time 90SU have been involved in every major conflict and operation that has taken place worldwide.

## 347

# ROYAL AUSTRALIAN AIR FORCE

**In line with the lime trees of Millennium Avenue are eucalyptus trees planted to represent local associations with 463/467 Squadrons Royal Australian Air Force.**

348

# ADJUTANT GENERAL'S CORPS COMMEMORATIVE GARDEN

**The Adjutant General's Corps was formed on 6 April 1992 and is one of the largest Corps in the British Army. The Corps is comprised of four branches and provides combat human resources specialists, Military Police, Military Provost Staff, Military Provost Guard service, educational and training services and Army legal services. Representatives of the Corps serve in every unit of the British Army.**

The commemorative garden design is based on a concept representing Winchester Cathedral, looking at and through the Cathedral's west elevation.

Walk through the tall trees at the entrance, which represent the portals of the west face of the Cathedral, to the centrepiece of the garden, a copper beech with its circular bench seat. The trees planted on the left and right represent the pillars either side of the main aisle, which in turn lead to the line of trees at the rear of the garden symbolic of the high screen.

349

# STAFFORDSHIRE REGIMENT

**The Staffords are an amalgamation of two famous and much loved Regiments, The South Staffordshire Regiment which was formed in 1705 in Lichfield, and The North Staffordshire Regiment which was formed in 1756. Both Regiments distinguished themselves in campaigns all over the world. In World War I they fought in all the main battles such as Mons, Loos, Somme and Ypres. In World War II, Staffordshire Battalions took part in heavy fighting in Dunkirk, Burma, Italy, Normandy and Arnhem.**

The Regiments amalgamated in 1959, and the Staffords served in the Ugandan Mutiny, Northern Ireland, the Gulf War, Kosovo and two tours in Iraq. They now form the 3rd Battalion The Mercian Regiment.

Famous people from the Staffords include William Coltman VC DCM* MM*, the most decorated soldier in the History of the British Army.

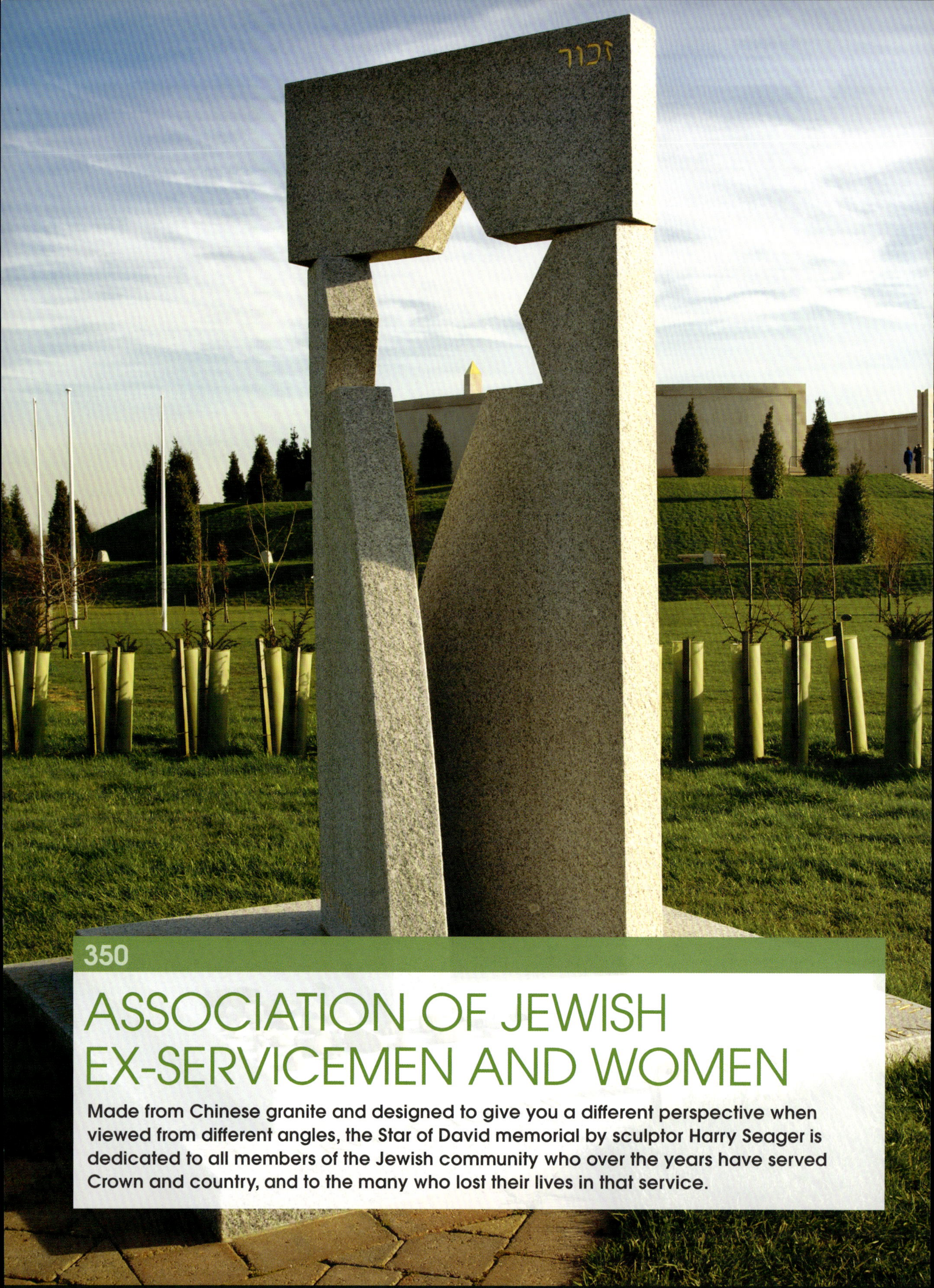


350

# ASSOCIATION OF JEWISH EX-SERVICEMEN AND WOMEN

**Made from Chinese granite and designed to give you a different perspective when viewed from different angles, the Star of David memorial by sculptor Harry Seager is dedicated to all members of the Jewish community who over the years have served Crown and country, and to the many who lost their lives in that service.**

## 350a

# THE SHRIEVALTY AVENUE

**Millennium Avenue incorporates a number of lime trees sponsored by High Sheriffs, some of whom were in office at the time of the Millennium.**

All these trees were propagated from the 2,000 year-old lime tree growing at Westonbirt Arboretum in Gloucestershire. This Millennium sponsorship by High Sheriffs was singularly appropriate given that the office of High Sheriff (or Shire Reeve) is at least 1,000 years old, having its roots in Saxon times well before the Norman Conquest of 1066. It is the oldest continuous secular office under the Crown. Originally a High Sheriff had vested in him many of the powers now vested in a Lord Lieutenant, High Court Judges and Magistrates. The office of High Sheriff remained first in precedence in the counties until King Edward VII by Order in Council in 1908 gave that primacy to the Lord Lieutenant. The High Sheriff remains the Sovereign's representative in a county for all matters relating to the Judiciary and to the maintenance of law and order. The involvement of the High Sheriffs in the Millennium Avenue underlines their service to their Sovereign and to the counties for more than a thousand years.

## 351

# GALLIPOLI

**This memorial remembers the terrible loss of life which occurred during World War I when a force famously including the Australian and New Zealand Army Corps (ANZAC) attempted to land and defeat the armies of the Ottoman Empire. They were attempting to capture Constantinople and secure a sea route to Russia. There were huge casualties on both sides.**

The monument includes a tree sculpture of dead oak trees, pollarded to represent the arms and hands of injured soldiers reaching upwards in hope of rescue as they lay in the mud among the unburied dead.

352

# MERCIAN VOLUNTEERS

**The Mercian Volunteers Regimental Association created the Mercian Grove in 2004 with four oak saplings and a stone memorial. It commemorates all those regular and Territorial Army (TA) soldiers who served with Mercian Volunteers and its constituent units between 1967 and 1988.**

For 21 years, its battalions were part of the British Army's contribution to NATO during the cold war and had a specific role in Germany. Its direct successor is the 4th Battalion The Mercian Regiment. Pte Luke Cole, one of its TA soldiers, was awarded the MC in 2007 whilst serving in Afghanistan.

353

# HOME SERVICE FORCE

**The memorial plinth with its surrounding trees, shrubs and plaques is dedicated to the HSF 1985–1992. The HSF was formed on 1 April 1985 as part of the Territorial Army (TA), although it is acknowledged that some units were formed on a trial basis earlier than this. Membership of the Home Service Force (HSF) was restricted to those who had previous service in the Armed Forces, or in the TA. 48 units were formed throughout the Country with each unit being attached to an existing Regular Army or TA, Regiment or Battalion for things such as administration and training.**

The HSF was given the task of guarding key installations in the United Kingdom such as major power stations and communication centres, the loss of which through subversive enemy action could have seriously affected the running of the Country. However in 1992 the threat that had necessitated the forming of HSF was considered to have diminished sufficiently to enable it to be disbanded.

# TOC H

**The name comes from a rest house for soldiers at Poperinge in Belgium about six miles from Ypres. Open from 1915 to the end of World War I it was run by Rev. 'Tubby' Clayton, an Australian and very jovial character.**

The home was given the name Talbot House in memory of Lieutenant Gilbert Talbot, killed in action, the brother of Rev Talbot who first had the idea for a rest home. It was open to all ranks, but rank had to be 'left at the door' because all men were equal once inside.

It became very popular, a haven of peace and safety away from the fighting, but was also described as "a lively pub without beer", and a chapel was built upstairs.

The famous lamp is an oil lamp used by Tubby Clayton. They do not give out much light, hence the saying "Dim as a TocH lamp", meaning not too clever. It is now called 'The Lamp of Maintenance'.

Post World War I, Toc H adopted the lamp as its symbol and the principles of fellowship, service, fair-mindedness and reconciliation. Branches existed in many countries around the world. Over the years it has followed its mission of healing the divisions of society through bringing people together and creating friendships between individuals.

In 2010 Toc H held a rededication following enhancements to the memorial.

# THE BLUE ZONE

**Access:** From Far East Walk and Millennium Avenue.

**Terrain:** Firm surface on Yeomanry Avenue and Millennium Avenue with rough mown grassland around and between the memorials and trees.

**Starting point:** Intersection of Far East Walk and Yeomanry Avenue.

"IT WAS A FANTASTIC, MEMORABLE DAY NOT ONLY FOR THE PUPILS BUT STAFF TOO. THEY HAVE REMEMBERED SO MUCH AFTER THE TRIP AND IT HAS ALSO MADE THEM THINK ABOUT THE EFFECTS OF CONFLICT."

The Croft Primary School, Armitage.

## 401

# YEOMANRY AVENUE

**This is an avenue of 48 large and small leaved lime trees where each tree is dedicated to a Yeomanry Unit. The Yeomanry were first raised as units of mounted volunteers during the Napoleonic Wars, to defend against invasion from abroad or revolution at home.**

In the 1790s, the threat of invasion of the Kingdom of Great Britain was high after the French Revolution and the rise of Napoleon Bonaparte. In order to improve the country's defences, volunteer regiments were raised in many counties from yeomen. The word 'yeoman' refers to small farmers who owned the land they cultivated, but the officers were drawn from the nobility and many of the men were their tenants. Yeomanry were not obliged to serve overseas without their individual consent.

During the first half of the nineteenth century, Yeomanry Regiments were used extensively in support of the civil authority to quell riots and civil disturbances (including the Peterloo Massacre), but as police forces took over this role, the Yeomanry concentrated on local defence.

During the Boer War, companies of The Imperial Yeomanry were formed from volunteers from the Yeomanry to serve overseas. In 1908, the Yeomanry became part of the Territorial Army.

Photo by Phil Nixon

## 401a

# BRITISH SOUTH AFRICA POLICE

**This regimental memorial replicates that which was erected in 1921 in the Morris Depot (the training depot for new recruits) in Salisbury, Rhodesia (now Harare, Zimbabwe). This was originally known as the Blatherwick Memorial, Jimmy Blatherwick being the most famous Regimental Sergeant Major, who died in 1918.**

The British South Africa Police (BSAP) was the Police Force of the British South Africa Company founded by Cecil Rhodes in 1889 to provide protection for the settlers. It became the Police Force of Southern Rhodesia (subsequently Rhodesia and now Zimbabwe).

The memorial was dedicated on 25 July 2010 and remembers all those who served in the British South Africa Police Force.

# 402

# ROYAL HONG KONG POLICE

**The Hong Kong Police Force was founded in 1844, when Hong Kong Island was ceded to Britain by China following the First Opium War.**

The first Police Officers were European and Indian ex-soldiers, together with some locally recruited Chinese. In 1845, Charles May, a former London Metropolitan Police Superintendent, took command of the 171-strong Force. Hong Kong grew in importance as a trading port, and following the Japanese Occupation during World War II, also as a manufacturing, financial and tourist centre. The Force was honoured with the title 'Royal' following very serious disturbances arising from the Cultural Revolution which took place in China in 1967. By 1997, when sovereignty of Hong Kong returned to China, the population of Hong Kong was some 6.5 million people, and the Force consisted of 28,000 regular Police Officers, with 5,700 Auxiliaries, and 6,000 civilian staff.

# 402a

# NORTHERN RHODESIA POLICE MEMORIAL

**This memorial commemorates all who served in the Northern Rhodesia Police from 1911 to 1964 and its predecessors the North Eastern Rhodesia Constabulary and Barotse Native Police, who suppressed the slave trade.**

It particularly remembers those who died on duty in Northern Rhodesia (now Zambia) or on active service in East Africa 1914 – 1918.

The memorial consists of a black granite stone on a light grey honed granite plinth with an incised silver line map and solid gilded area showing Northern Rhodesia.

# 403

# BIDADARI CEMETERY

**The four cherry trees commemorate the Bidadari Christian Cemetery which contains the graves of people who died in Singapore from 1908 to 1972. Today, Bidadari Cemetery is no longer in use, and most of the graves have been exhumed to allow land redevelopment.**

## 403a

# MEMORIAL FOR ST JOHN VOLUNTEERS

**The garden has been designed to commemorate the thousands of volunteers who have helped the charity over the years in its mission to provide first aid in many different situations.**

The Duke of Gloucester, who is the Grand Prior of the Order of St John, officially opened the memorial in 2009. The design of the memorial takes the form of the St John (Amalfi) Cross. The entrance is through one of the arms of the cross which is flanked by two granite panels depicting the badge of St John and the Priory of England and the Islands. At the centre of the cross is a black granite stone with the inscription: "In honour of all those who have faithfully served the Venerable Order of the Hospital of St John of Jerusalem and its foundations".

## 404

# BLESMA EXTENSION

**The 70 fruit trees – of varieties Bramley Seedling, Fiesta, James Grieve, Golden Delicious, Cox's Orange Pippin, Katie and Egremont Russet – are dedicated to the service personnel of the British Limbless Ex-servicemen's Association (BLESMA).**

## 405

# YANGTZE INCIDENT

**The circular planting of 46 Chinese euonymus plants commemorates each life lost during the Yangtze Incident in China in 1949.**

A plaque alongside the memorial tells the full story of the Yangtze Incident. Inside the circle are a black polished granite monument and trees planted as a tribute to HMS Amethyst, HMS Black Swan, HMS Consort and HMS London which were the four ships involved in the incident. The human cost in the four ships was 46 dead and 68 injured. The tree planted just outside the circle remembers the RAF Sunderland flying boat named D-DOG ML772 from 88 Squadron that, on the fourth attempt, landed successfully on the Yangtze River alongside HMS Amethyst to deliver medical supplies and a replacement doctor.

## 406

# ROYAL INDIAN NAVY AND INDIAN ARMY

**Between the Yangtze Incident and Far East Air Force memorials, trees from the Indian sub-continent such as Kashmir rowan, cedar and Bhutan pine have been planted as a tribute to those who served in the Royal Indian Navy (1934-1947) and Indian Army. The British Indian Army (1858–1947) was a force recruited locally during the British Colonisation of India and commanded by expatriate British officers.**

## 407

# FAR EAST AIR FORCE

**Dedicated in 2006, this memorial comprising 42 hand engraved Lakeland slate tiles commemorates the history of the Royal Air Force from 1948 to 1971, when the RAF was engaged in assisting the Malays through Confrontation and a period of Emergency.**

Malaysia gained independence in 1957 and Singapore separated from Malaysia in 1965. As both nations developed their own Armed Forces, the RAF reduced its commitment and withdrew in 1971.

The Units listed on the memorial were the backbone of operations and provided bases for strategic reinforcement to the Far East, should it have been required.

## 408

# DIAMOND GROVE

**The trees in the Diamond Grove have been sponsored by couples from the Second World War generation to celebrate 60 years of marriage, their Diamond Wedding anniversary.**

409

# ROYAL NORWEGIAN NAVY

**This avenue holds native species of silver birch trees from Norway together with memorial plaques, all sponsored by the Royal Norwegian Navy and commemorating Norway's important involvement in protecting the Merchant Convoys of World War II.**

409a

# NATIONAL ASSOCIATION OF MEMORIAL MASONS

**The Association was formed in 1907 to promote excellence and craftsmanship within the memorial masonry trade. Through its strict codes of business practice and working practice National Association of Memorial Masons (NAMM) demands the very highest standards of its members.**

The NAMM exhibition was created to provide a permanent marker to celebrate 100 years of service to both its members and bereaved families. It is a timeline of memorialisation from Stone Age to the present day. The garden also aims to encourage children to understand how history, Remembrance and heritage is linked to memorialisation.

The exhibition, designed as a Centenary Garden was officially opened by HRH The Princess Royal on 20 May 2008.

410

# FLEET AIR ARM OFFICERS

Photo by Roger Hallwood

**In 2009 the Royal Navy celebrated the Centenary of Naval aviation and the memorial honours the sacrifice made by the 6,749 men and women who gave their lives in the service of Naval aviation over the preceding 100 years.**

Over 80% of front line Fleet Air Arm Squadrons are currently deployed on operations around the world including Afghanistan. The memorial is a sculptured plinth of Portland stone supporting a granite aircraft carrier.

410a

# ROYAL MARINES ASSOCIATION

**This memorial is of Dartmoor granite to represent the one part of the country that most Royal Marines will associate with their training. It is the only Corps where all training is conducted at the same place from recruits through all ranks to officers. The Corps has fought in all conflicts since World War II and many brave men and their families are remembered in this reflective place.**

Any family that wishes to place a brass plaque on the benches so that a loved one is remembered by name can do so through the Royal Marines Association.

411

# BRITISH NUCLEAR TEST VETERANS

**Formed in 1983, the Association is a focus for the men who served at the test sites and combines comradeship with the objective of recognition of the ill effects suffered by some veterans.**

Beginning in 1952 and continuing until 1965 there were 21 major British nuclear tests and numerous minor tests at the sites listed on the memorial. The Association has about 1,400 members of which one third are widows. Membership is limited to men who served, their widows and descendants.

The memorial (grotto) is a replica of a shell-decorated memorial situated on Christmas Island where some of the British nuclear tests took place.

411a

# THE COMMANDOS

**The British Commandos were first formed by the Army in June 1940 during World War II as a well-armed but non-regimental raider force employing unconventional and irregular tactics to assault, disrupt and reconnoitre the enemy in mainland Europe and Scandinavia.**

Initially raids were made by comparatively small numbers, were of short duration and at night, later growing in complexity and size. The Commandos were formed and operated in secrecy and produced a demoralising effect on German coastal forces while achieving celebrity status among the British public, comparable with that attached to fighter pilots, and shrouded in myth. As the war progressed Commandos operated increasingly in the role of shock troops, sometimes up to brigade strength and sometimes in conjunction with infantry.

This memorial consists of a reproduction of part of the Association badge – the wreath in copper and the Fairbairn-Sykes fighting knife in stainless steel. The impressive piece was created at Anwick Forge in Lincolnshire and dedicated in the presence of HRH Prince Philip, The Duke of Edinburgh, in July 2007.

## 411b

# SHROPSHIRE YEOMANRY MEMORIAL PLINTH

**The memorial was dedicated on Saturday 13 March 2010 by Colonel Evans, President of the Association. It was built by Bob Sadler after a buy-a-brick scheme organised with Association members to raise funds. The central plaque was produced by stone mason John Beer.**

### Private Harold Whitfield VC

"On 10 March 1918 at Buji El Lisaneh, Egypt, during the first of three counter-attacks made by the enemy on the position which had just been captured by his battalion, Private Whitfield single-handedly charged and captured a Lewis gun, killed the whole gun team and turned the gun on the enemy, driving them back with heavy casualties. Later he organised and led a bombing attack on the enemy, again inflicting many casualties, and by establishing his party in their position saved many lives and materially assisted in the defeat of the counter-attack."

## 412

# THE ANTELOPE GARDEN

**The Antelope Garden commemorates the 25th anniversary in 2007 of the Falklands Campaign, and particularly the loss of HMS Antelope. The location of the garden at the junction of the RAF, Army and Royal Naval memorial plots is particularly significant as this was a tri-service campaign. The garden was opened on 2 April 2007 by Captain Nick Tobin, the former Commanding Officer of HMS Antelope. It is planted with Viscosa Antelope, a deciduous azalea which produces pink fragrant flowers with a faint yellow blotch in May.**

Nearby is a tree planted by Lady Fieldhouse in memory of her husband Admiral of the Fleet Lord Fieldhouse, of Gosport in the County of Hampshire. As Commander in Chief Fleet in 1982, John Fieldhouse was the Commander of the Task Force, and given responsibility for 'Operation Corporate', the mission to recover the Falkland Islands. There is also a bench dedicated to the South Atlantic Medal Association.

413

# ROYAL NAVAL REVIEW

**The collection of oak trees interspersed with a number of memorial plinths and plaques dedicated to individual Royal Naval ships and Associations forms the Royal Naval Review. Groups remembered here include the Submariners (whose plinth shows images and details of their 14 VC holders), the Royal Naval Air Service and the Royal Marine Commandos.**

The Loch Class Frigate memorial cairn is dedicated to the ships' companies who served aboard the Loch Class Frigates and their variants in World War II and all theatres up to 1970. The cairn includes stones from each of the Scottish lochs after which the Frigates were named.

## HMS NEPTUNE & HMS KANDAHAR ASSOCIATION

**In December 1941 HMS Kandahar together with the cruiser HMS Neptune were sunk by mines in the Mediterranean with the massive loss of just over 900 lives.**

The tragedy was the second most substantial loss of life suffered by the Royal Navy in the whole of the Mediterranean campaign and ranks among the heaviest crew losses experienced in any naval theatre of World War II.

The pyramid shaped HMS Kandahar and HMS Neptune memorial is positioned so that it aligns with the exact position off the coast of Libya from Tripoli where the wreck of HMS Neptune lies. Concealed within the stone blocks of the memorial are a roll of honour of the 800 men who died and a painting of the night sky as it was on the day of the sinking. An unknown number of survivors tried to swim to safety, but due to rough seas and darkness only one of the crew of 765 survived.

## ARTIFICER APPRENTICES OF HMS CALEDONIA 1937 – 1985

**Artificers have served in the Royal Navy since 1868. They were the men who repaired and maintained all the equipment on His or Her Majesty's ships wherever they were in the world. They kept the engines turning, the guns firing, and the ships floating, the electrical equipment working and the aircraft flying.**

To reach high levels of skill Artificers have to successfully complete a four year apprenticeship and HMS Caledonia was where many Artificers were trained.

## CAPTAIN CLASS FRIGATE ASSOCIATION

**In September 1940 after approaches by British Prime Minister Winston Churchill, the President of the USA Franklin D. Roosevelt authorised the exchange of 50 former World War I four stack flush deck destroyers from the US Navy reserve fleet. Orders for 50 units were placed with four ship yards in November 1941 at Boston, Mare Island, Philadelphia and Puget Sound. Most were named after Lord Nelson's senior officers and captains, and the final 10 ships were named after ships of World War I.**

## HMS HOOD ASSOCIATION

The memorial commemorates the 1,415 men lost in the sinking of HMS Hood on 24 May 1941. It was dedicated on 25 October 2008.

## HMS GANGES ASSOCIATION

After nearly 40 years based on the last wooden walled sea-going flag ship, HMS Ganges, the training of Boy Seamen was transferred ashore in 1905 to Shotley, near Ipswich, Suffolk. The establishment, which was later renamed HMS Ganges (a name that goes back 250 years), was opened as a Boy Seaman's training school accepting boys between the ages of 15 and 16 and a half. The establishment was closed in 1976 following the raising of the school leaving age to 17 and initial training of all Naval Ratings transferred to HMS Raleigh in Cornwall. Two Boys went on to win the VC, one in World War I and the other in World War II.

413a

# ROYAL NAVAL PATROL SERVICE

**The Royal Naval Patrol Service (RNPS) was set up in August 1939. Consisting initially of 200 trawlers, drifters and whalers manned by some 6,000 fishermen, the ships were equipped with guns mostly from World War I and with anti-submarine patrol and minesweeping equipment. By the end of the war there were 66,000 men, 600 Wrens and 2,000 ships.**

Minesweeping activities were vital to the task of keeping open the shipping lanes around the United Kingdom and further afield. The RNPS was involved in the Norway Campaign where Captain (then Lieutenant) Richard Stannard won the Victoria Cross while in command of HMT Arab being attacked from the air at Namsos.

Thousands of troops were ferried back to the UK from Dunkirk by ships of the RNPS. The trawler HMT Cambridgeshire rescued many from the bombing of HMT Lancastria in the estuary of the River Loire and then returned the same night to pick up the Commander of the British Expeditionary Force, Lieutenant-General Alan Brooke and his staff because his original destroyer transport was no longer available.

As the war developed the RNPS could be found in many naval theatres – from the eastern seaboard of the USA where refitted trawlers were lost to the U-boats they were searching for, to the Mediterranean where HMT Moonstone captured the Italian submarine 'Galileo Galilei'. In 1944 235 minesweepers swept the Channel ahead of the invasion fleet.

The bravery of 'Harry Tate's Navy' or 'Churchill's pirates', as they had come to be known, is told by their losses – over 5,000 men perished, 2,385 with no known grave but the sea, and 475 ships never returned to port.

Photo copyright National Memorial Arboretum

414

# DEFENSIVELY EQUIPPED MERCHANT SHIPS

**In the centre of the Defensively Equipped Merchant Ships (DEMS) memorial garden is a Bofors gun of the type which were fitted on merchant ships and manned by Maritime Royal Artillery gunners.**

The garden is dedicated to the impressive wartime record of the DEMS personnel. In all 27,680 officers and ratings passed gunnery and defensive equipment courses. DEMS gunners, an integral part of the Royal Navy, were deployed on merchant ships in numbers varying from two on the smallest ships up to 100 in the larger transporters. Sacrifices were heavy with 2,713 gunners killed or missing.

415

# MASTER MARINERS SUNDIAL

**The 20 foot (six metre) diameter 'human' sundial was designed by Christopher St J H Daniel and executed in situ by Mark Frith in Dunhouse stone and blue Elterwater slate.**

It was presented by the Honourable Company of Master Mariners and dedicated in 2001 to commemorate the loss of 2,535 ships of the Merchant Navy and the 32,000 merchant seamen who gave their lives in World War II. The dial represents an oval outline chart of the world and the shadow of a person standing on the date scale indicates the time (GMT) on the surrounding numbers.

# THE MERCHANT NAVY CONVOY

**The Convoy is dedicated to over 46,000 British merchant seafarers and fishermen lost in conflict during the 20th Century, including two World Wars, Falklands, Kuwait, Vietnam, Iran, Iraq and others.**

In World War II 31,908 seafarers perished, proportionately more than any of the Armed Services. 2,535 trees represent the British vessels lost at that time. Their ships carried cargo, troops, armaments, ammunition and fuel to every theatre of war. They were civilians who faced the enemy and the sea with equal bravery and fortitude, to keep the supply lines open to Britain and its allies.

## HMT LANCASTRIA

**A simple stone memorial is located in front of the 'Lancastria Oak' within the Merchant Navy Woodland bearing a circular plaque inscribed with the Lancastria Association badge and emblem.**

On 17 June 1940 the 16,000 ton Cunard liner Lancastria lay five miles off St Nazaire embarking troops, RAF personnel, and civilian refugees, including women and children, who were being evacuated from France, which was then on the point of collapse. The exact number on board may never be known, but almost certainly exceeded 6,000; some estimates were as high as 9,000. The Lancastria was attacked and hit by bombs from German aircraft. The ship sank rapidly and, according to the estimate of the Captain, only around 2,500 of those on board were saved.

Because of the scale of the tragedy, Winston Churchill forbade publication of the news, in the interests of public morale, and hence the story of the Lancastria has never been generally known, although it is Britain's worst maritime disaster.

416a

# ROYAL FLEET AUXILIARY SHIP 'SIR PERCIVALE' ANCHOR

**The central glade of the Merchant Navy Convoy is an appropriate home to one of the anchors from Royal Fleet Auxiliary (RFA) Sir Percivale which has been donated by the Merchant Navy Welfare Board.**

Outside the two World Wars the largest loss of Merchant Navy lives was during the Falklands conflict. Sir Percivale landed troops in San Carlos Bay and was the first British vessel to enter Port Stanley following the Argentinian surrender. She later served in the Gulf War of 1991, was deployed in support of British operations in the Balkans and was present at the handover of Hong Kong to China. She was crewed throughout her life by officers and ratings of the Merchant Navy.

The anchor was dedicated on 8 June 2011, the anniversary of the bombing of Sir Percivale's sister ships Sir Galahad and Sir Tristram in Bluff Cove during the Falklands conflict in 1982.

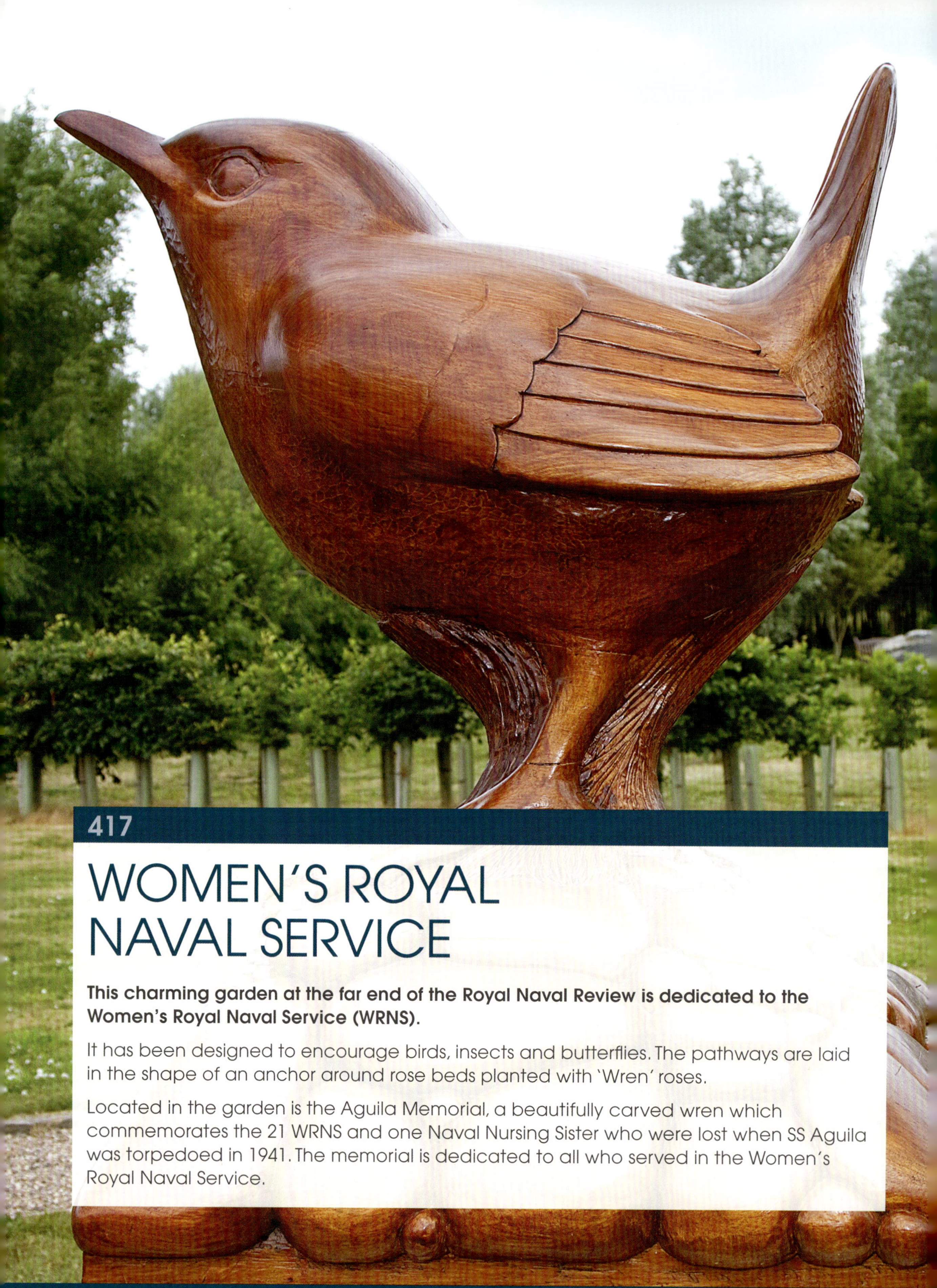

417

# WOMEN'S ROYAL NAVAL SERVICE

**This charming garden at the far end of the Royal Naval Review is dedicated to the Women's Royal Naval Service (WRNS).**

It has been designed to encourage birds, insects and butterflies. The pathways are laid in the shape of an anchor around rose beds planted with 'Wren' roses.

Located in the garden is the Aguila Memorial, a beautifully carved wren which commemorates the 21 WRNS and one Naval Nursing Sister who were lost when SS Aguila was torpedoed in 1941. The memorial is dedicated to all who served in the Women's Royal Naval Service.

## 417a

# ARMY DOG UNIT (NORTHERN IRELAND) ASSOCIATION RED PAW

**This memorial was dedicated on 1 August 2009 to the memory of those, both humans and animals, who lost their lives whilst serving in the Army Dog Unit, Northern Ireland.**

It is made from polished black granite designed in a wedge shape with an engraved face. The PAW graphics and words "Search and Secure" are the Association's motto.

## 417b

# THE QUEEN ALEXANDRA'S ROYAL NAVAL NURSING SERVICE AND THE VOLUNTARY AID DETACHMENT (RN)

**At the corner of the Merchant Navy Convoy and the Ulster Ash Grove, a blue pearl granite tablet is dedicated to all who served, and continue to serve, in The Queen Alexandra's Royal Naval Nursing Service (QARNNS) and the Voluntary Aid Detachment (RN).**

Matching curved benches are flanked each side by a rowan tree, known as the 'healing' tree. Its berries are used for medical purposes and its wood was used to make handles for stretchers during World War I.

# ULSTER SPECIAL CONSTABULARY

**The black marble and blue limestone monument was dedicated on 29 July 2006 as a tribute to 50 years of public-spirited service on the part of the Ulster Special Constabulary.**

Formed in October 1920 by Sir Ernest Clark, Additional Assistant Under-secretary in the Irish Office, the new Special Constabulary comprised three categories. Firstly the 'A' Specials who were paid and worked full-time with the same arms and equipment as the Royal Ulster Constabulary, secondly the 'B' Specials who were part-time and unpaid apart from a small allowance for clothing and whose arms were determined by the police county commander, and thirdly the 'C' Specials, a reserve force called out in emergencies. By the end of 1920 the Ulster Special Constabulary totalled 3,500 'A', 16,000 'B' and over 1,000 'C' Constables. The Ulster Special Constabulary was stood down on 30 April 1970.

## 418a

# THE ROYAL BRITISH LEGION NATIONAL REMEMBRANCE GARDEN – 'MY REMEMBRANCE DAY'

**My Remembrance Day is a unique and personal memorial where a sponsor chooses the date on which they want to remember a loved one and an everlasting poppy is dedicated to that person's memory. The wooden poppy, bearing the name of the person being remembered, is then planted in the circular bed in a segment for the month in which their relatives and friends wish to remember them.**

## 419

# ARMED SERVICES WOOD

**A woodland of mixed trees individually sponsored as living tributes to those who served in the British Army, The Royal Navy and the Royal Air Force.**

419a

# DOUGLAS SKENE GROVE

**Douglas Skene (1948 – 2007) was a dedicated military historian, a serving officer in the Royal Scots Greys and a member of the Territorial Army with the Royal Green Jackets. He practiced as an independent financial consultant but his hobby was to lead tours to World War I battlefields. His other great love was trees and he enjoyed watching the Arboretum develop from its inception until his untimely death at the age of 59. Following his death his family, friends and colleagues raised funds towards setting up the first grove of specimen trees at the Arboretum, a lasting legacy to his memory,**

Trees in the Grove include Berberis valdiviana, the barberry from Chile; Aesculus flava, the sweet buckeye from South-East USA; Cupressus funebris, the Chinese weeping cypress from central China; Cornus kousa, the dogwood from Japan/Korea.

420

# THE ULSTER ASH GROVE

**The Ulster Ash Grove has been planted as a living tribute to the members of the Royal Ulster Constabulary GC, the Royal Ulster Constabulary Reserve, the Armed Forces and other organisations in the service of the crown, who lost their lives during the troubles in Northern Ireland between 1969 and 2001.**

The weeping ash trees planted within the grove represent lives lost in the cause of peace in Northern Ireland and form an ever-changing backdrop to the stone circle and Mourne granite pillar. The circle contains one block of stone quarried from each of the six counties and are placed to form a symbolic map of Northern Ireland. The Ulster Grove memorial was dedicated on 23 September 2003, the anniversary of the death of the first soldier in 1969.

## 420a

# THE RUC GC WAY

**The Royal Ulster Constabulary George Cross Way was designed in memory of the Royal Ulster Constabulary police officers who lost their lives whilst protecting life and property, preventing and detecting crime and keeping the community safe in Northern Ireland from 1922 - 2001.**

The Juniper trees lining the Way represent the 38 Sub-Divisional policing areas of the Province in which the officers worked and were killed or injured while carrying out their duties.

## 421

# THE HOME FRONT

**Home Front is the informal term commonly used to describe the civilian populace of the nation at war as an active support system of its military. The large quarried stone with a memorial plaque was dedicated on 20 May 2006 as a tribute to those who worked on the home front to support the war effort from 1939 to 1945. The people of Burton-on-Trent, including the Fire Service, donated the memorial.**

## 421a

# THE NATIONAL EX-PRISONER OF WAR ASSOCIATION

**A memorial dedicated to the memory of those who fell by the wayside on the many routes from Polish POW camps was built in Fallingbostel, Germany, by members of 2 Battn REME.**

Veterans of those journeys marched in appalling conditions. Many suffered diseases such as typhoid and diphtheria or carried wounds inflicted prior to or after capture. All were malnourished and had inadequate clothing and equipment to protect them during one of Germany's worst recorded winters. The memorial here was also built by members of 2 Battn REME and Royal Engineers and is an exact replica of the one in Fallingbostel. It is dedicated to the memory of those made prisoner in World War II theatres in Scandinavia, Europe, the Middle East and North Africa.

422 F Map reference

# THE CHILDREN'S WOODLAND

**Sponsored by the Midlands Co-operative Society Limited and planted with 2,640 native British trees, the Children's Woodland was designed to combine arboriculture and wildlife education with Remembrance.**

Individual trees have been sponsored by families and schools and dedicated to babies and children who have passed away. In the nearby shelter are large child-sized wooden figures of the characters from 'The Wind in the Willows' by Kenneth Grahame, carved by the Essex Woodcarvers under the supervision of Peter Benson, Chairman of the Master Woodcarvers Association.

## THE WOODLAND ACTIVITY AREA

**The Arboretum children's activity area and picnic area was funded by Staffordshire Aggregates Levy Grant Scheme (SALGS). It is a purpose-built wooden environment for children aged between 7–13 years.**

## 422a

# THE EDWARDS TRUST GARDEN

**The Edwards Trust is a charity that provides bereavement services to children and families.**

Designed by Hannah Genders, The Edwards Trust Garden aims to immediately connect people with the garden and its purpose. The design of the tree, sculpted by David Watkinson, and surrounding area pays attention to the grief experience. Fundamental to this are the symbols of 'hope' and the importance of care and support to those who grieve.

The garden has won two British Association of Landscape Industries (BALI) Awards – landscape design excellence award and a special award for innovative design.

## 423

# FELLOWSHIP OF THE SERVICES

**In this peaceful setting alongside the River Tame, 114 trees have been planted as a living tribute to the Fellowship of the Services and to keep alive the memory of the individual Messes who have sponsored the grove.**

A Brotherhood of officers and men, Fellowship is the underlying spirit of comradeship proved in the fires of two World Wars and perpetuated in a 'Brotherhood' of ex-servicemen drawn from all ranks of HM Forces. The majority are officers and men who served in these wars and carry on a Service Brotherhood, an association created out of the unforgettable experiences of World War I.

Photo by Phil Nixon

## 424

# MILLENNIUM WOOD

**A woodland of individually sponsored mixed variety trees with Remembrance plaques and labels.**

424a

# WOMEN'S INSTITUTE

**The Women's Institute (WI) dry stone wall with seats was designed and built by Derbyshire's only registered female dry stonewaller, Sally Hodgson. The stone was donated by Longcliffe Quarry, Brassington.**

The curving wall includes seats facing in two directions, one side looking out at the River Tame and the other along the beautiful meadow planted with poppies and wild flowers.

The dedication, on 22 June 2009, was attended by the Dowager Duchess of Devonshire, a past Patron of the National Dry Stone Walling Association and a member of the WI for over 75 years.

# THE ROYAL BRITISH LEGION POPPY FIELD

**The Royal British Legion is a leading Service and ex-Service organisation and one of the UK's most established and respected charities. Its principal concern is the welfare of ex-Service personnel and their dependants, with around 11 million people in the UK eligible for that support.**

The Royal British Legion Avenue is a 200m grove lined with 44 5m tall English oaks. Poppy seeds have been sown between the oaks to initiate the Poppy Field which will gradually become self-seeding and will create a stunning feature in May and June each year. As they grow, the avenue of oaks will become a dramatic feature giving a tree-lined vista across the site when viewed from next to the wartime pillbox on the bank of the River Tame.

## 425a

# THE SPIRITUALISTS NATIONAL UNION

**The memorial was dedicated on Saturday 10 July 2010 in memory of Spiritualists who have served and continue to serve in the British and Commonwealth Armed Forces, and all Spiritualists who have served their country in times of conflict.**

The memorial comprises a circular bench made from polished beige granite topped with curved coping slabs to form a seat. Within the bench are seven curved pieces of Balmoral red granite, each one bearing symbolic words.

The internal floor of the circle is paved with the same two types of granite, depicting a seven pointed star. Standing in the centre of the circle is an obelisk with a pyramid top.

## 426

# RAC FUTURE FORESTS

**Future Forests is a scheme that measures emissions of carbon dioxide, the greenhouse gas which scientists think is responsible for global warming. The scheme helps to offset this pollution by planting natural forests and woodlands and investing in renewable energy.**

The Royal Automobile Club (RAC) Future Forests wood was sponsored by the RAC as part of the Future Forests scheme and as a tribute to their employees who have now retired.

## 427

# THE ROADPEACE WOOD

**The memorial has been designed to represent a circular tarmac traffic island with the RoadPeace insignia of a dove and a memorial plaque in the centre.**

The memorial with its individually sponsored trees and benches is in memory of victims of road accidents and has been sponsored by RoadPeace, a charity that supports people who have suffered bereavement or injury through road accidents.

428

# ALLIED SPECIAL FORCES ASSOCIATION

**The Allied Special Forces Association (ASFA) is dedicated to creating the Allied Special Forces Memorial Grove which is a tribute to the bravery and courage of all who served in or assisted the Allied Special Forces and Resistance Units during World War II and in many of the conflicts since.**

The ASFA's link with the past is a tree seat dedicated to John McCrae the Canadian Doctor who penned the poem 'In Flanders Fields'. It is as evocative today as it was in 1915.

In 2010 a new plaque was dedicated to two agents of the Special Operations Executive; Humphrey McCare of the Dutch SOE and David Finlayson of the French SOE. Both were captured on landing after being betrayed by enemy agents and both suffered horrific torture and eventual execution in Gross Rosen concentration camp in 1944.

During World War II Special Operations enlisted thousands of individuals capable of working in enemy territory. Men, women and supplies were dropped by, among others, Maurice Davis who as part of 299 Squadron RAF managed along with his crew to survive the war intact. Once these agents were in place they communicated with the Special Operations Executive Signals department to arrange more supplies, help and agents. These agents along with locally recruited men, women and children of the resistance forces helped liberate the occupied countries.

429

# WESTERN FRONT ASSOCIATION

**The Western Front Association (WFA) is an historical interest group established in 1980 by noted military historian John Giles which has a worldwide membership of over 6,500. The WFA supports many Remembrance and research projects, including the renovation of battlefield memorials.**

At the time of publication of this edition of the Guidebook, the WFA memorial is still being planned and developed, although some hornbeams propagated from the only tree in Delville Wood to survive the Battle of the Somme have been planted. The Commonwealth War Graves Commission supplied the trees and most are individually dedicated.

430

# UNITED NATIONS AVENUE

**This is an avenue of giant redwoods planted alongside the mainline railway bridge, which will be clearly visible from passing trains as the trees grow.**

Member countries of the United Nations have sponsored the trees and plaques.

Photo by David McDonnell

431

# WATERSMEET

**Watersmeet is a native British riverside wood comprising silver birch, black poplar and willow between the railway bridge and the confluence of the rivers Tame and Trent. The woodland was planted with the assistance of the International Tree Foundation's Family Tree Scheme and encompasses both Lovejoy Wood and Mac's Wood which celebrate the lives of Professor Derek Lovejoy and Meg Carroll respectively.**

Nearby is the recently constructed Mythaholme Footbridge. The bridge was installed by the Central Rivers Initiative, a partnership to ensure the successful regeneration of this section of the Trent and Tame valleys after quarrying. Mythaholme is an Old English word meaning 'the space between the merging of two rivers'.

# SUPPORTING THE ARBORETUM

**As a charity the Arboretum relies on the generous support of individuals and organisations to maintain this unique and special free-entry site of national significance.**

Help us continue to grow and improve the Arboretum, enabling more families and colleagues to remember the sacrifice of loved ones in this spiritually uplifting place. We are grateful for all gifts, large or small, which make it possible to continue our vital work.

# DONATIONS

## REGULAR GIVING

**A regular gift to the Arboretum, large or small, enables us to plan for the future. Please support us in this special way and help more visitors, both young and old, benefit from this special place of Remembrance.**

## NATIONAL MEMORIAL ARBORETUM FRIENDS

**Become a Friend today and support the Arboretum with a regular gift, either monthly or annually, whilst benefitting from a quarterly newsletter and increased involvement with the Arboretum. You can join by calling us on 01283 792 333 or emailing friends@thenma.org.uk. Alternatively, download a membership application from our website.**

## FUNDRAISE FOR US

**Why not have a car boot sale, run a race, bake cakes or host a quiz.**

There are many ways to organise an event to raise money for the Arboretum.

To receive our fundraising pack with lots of ideas, call us on 01283 792 333 or visit our website.

Don't forget to create your own Just Giving page and visit ours **www.justgiving/thenma** to collate online donations.

## STANDING ORDER

Setting up a monthly donation by standing order makes supporting the Arboretum easier, and even reduces our administration costs. **Please contact the Arboretum's finance department for further information.**

## SINGLE GIFT

**Cheque**

If you would like to support us by sending a cheque our address is: National Memorial Arboretum, Croxall Road, Alrewas, Staffordshire DE13 7AR.

**Credit Card**

Call us on 01283 792 333 and make a donation over the phone; a member of staff will be happy to talk you through the procedure.

**Website**

To donate online please visit our website: www.thenma.org.uk

## GIFT AID

**Please don't forget to make your gift worth 25% more, at no extra cost to you!**

If you are a UK tax payer, and pay an amount of Income Tax and/or Capital Gains Tax at least equal to the tax the charity reclaims on your behalf, the National Memorial Arboretum can increase the value of your donation by 25%. If you are a UK tax payer and would like us to reclaim the tax on your donation, please complete a gift aid form which is available on request.

## LEGACIES

**Remember the Arboretum in your will and help keep loving memories alive for future generations.**

By leaving a gift in your will you can enable the National Memorial Arboretum to continue its vital work for future generations to enjoy and remember. Making a gift in your will means your generous support and commitment to Remembrance can continue long after your lifetime. Legacy donations are a vital source of funding and any gift will be put to excellent use at the Arboretum.

To find out more about remembering the National Memorial Arboretum in your will, or to let us know you have already done so (in order that we may thank you appropriately), please contact us on 01283 792 333 or email info@thenma.org.uk.

# DONATION FORM & INFORMATION

## YOUR CONTACT DETAILS:

Title:........................ Surname:............................................

Forenames:........................................................................

Address:...........................................................................

.......................................................................................

.......................................................................................

Postcode:.........................................................................

Telephone:........................................................................

Email:...............................................................................

## PLEASE LET US KNOW WHAT INFORMATION YOU WOULD LIKE TO RECEIVE

Leaflets and forms for
(please tick the items you would like to receive):

- Joining the Friends ☐
- Group Booking or Events ☐
- Leaving a Legacy ☐
- Making a Donation ☐
- Fundraising or Sponsorship ☐
- Volunteering ☐

## DONATION (OPTIONAL):

I enclose a donation of £..............................................
Please make cheques payable to the **National Memorial Arboretum** and sign the Gift Aid declaration if you are able to.

## WHAT SHOULD I DO WITH THIS FORM?

Once you have filled out all the details simply cut free of the guide book, or photocopy the page, and either:

1. Hand it to one of our members of staff on reception, or
2. Place it in an envelope and post to us at: National Memorial Arboretum, Croxall Road, Alrewas, Staffordshire, DE13 7AR

## DONATE ONLINE:

Alternatively you could donate online at http://www.thenma.org.uk/get-involved/donation/

**GIFT AID DECLARATION**

giftaid it

**Gift Aid (paid to us by the Government) increases a donation of £100 to £125***
Declaration: "I wish you to treat as Gift Aid all donations that I make to the National Memorial Arboretum, Charity No. 1043992, from now until I notify otherwise. I understand that my donations are eligible to be treated as Gift Aid if I pay an amount of UK Income Tax or Capital Gains Tax at least equal to my Gift Aid donations in the tax year."
Signed ...............................................

Date ....................................................

*Accurate at time of print.

# THANK YOU!

**We need £3,745**
every day to ensure
the Arboretum is
free to enter

# ALPHABETICAL MEMORIAL INDEX

# ALPHABETICAL MEMORIAL INDEX

# ALPHABETICAL MEMORIAL INDEX

# ALPHABETICAL MEMORIAL INDEX

# ALPHABETICAL MEMORIAL INDEX

# NATIONAL MEMORIAL ARBORETUM

## Where our Nation remembers

All information in this Guidebook was accurate at time of print.

All photographs, unless otherwise stated, by Barry Turner.

Design by oceanbarefoot.

Printed by Andus Print Ltd.

The Arboretum would like to give special thanks to everyone who contributed their photographs to this Guidebook.
In particular, we thank Barry Turner for his generosity and continued support.

IS DEDICATED TO
AND RIFLEMEN OF
GREEN JACKETS
JANUARY